SEMINAR STUDIES IN HISTORY

General Editor: Roger Lockyer

Louis XIV 1661–1715

Peter Robert Campbell

LONGMAN
London and New York

Longman Group UK Limited,
Longman House, Burnt Mill, Harlow,
Essex CM20 2JE, England
and Associated Companies throughout the world.

Published in the United States of America
by Longman Inc., New York.

First published 1993

Set in 10/11 point Baskerville (Linotron)
Printed in Malaysia

ISBN 0 582 01770-X

British Library Cataloguing in Publication Data
Campbell, Peter Robert
  Louis XIV, 1661–1715.
  – (Seminar Studies in History)
  I. Title II. Series
  944.033092

  ISBN 0-582-01770-X

Library of Congress Cataloging-in-Publication Data
Campbell, Peter Robert, 1955–
  Louis XIV, 1661–1715/Peter Robert Campbell.
    p. cm. – (Seminar studies in history)
  Includes bibliographical references and index.
  ISBN 0–582–01770–X : £4.75
  1. Louis XIV, King of France, 1638–1715. 2. France – Kings and
rulers – Biography. 3. France – Politics and government – 1643–1715.
I. Title. II. Title: Louis 14th, 1661–1715. III. Title: Louis Fourteenth,
1661–1715. IV. Series.
DC128.C28 1993.
944'.033'092–dc20
[B]   92–42084
                                                                              CIP

Contents

Contents

Seminar Studies in History

Introduction to the series

Under the editorship of a reputable historian, Seminar Studies in History covers major themes in British and European history. The authors are acknowledged experts in their field and the volumes are works of scholarship in their own right as well as providing a survey of current historical interpretations. They are constantly updated, to take account of the latest research.

Each title has a brief introduction or background to the subject, a substantial section of analysis, followed by an assessment, a documents section and a bibliography as a guide to further study. The documents enable the reader to see how historical judgements are reached and also to question and challenge them.

The material is carefully selected to give the advanced student sufficient confidence to handle different aspects of the theme as well as being enjoyable and interesting to read. In short, Seminar Studies offer clearly written authoritative and stimulating introductions to important topics, bridging the gap between the general textbook and the specialised monograph.

Seminar Studies in History was the creation of Patrick Richardson, a gifted and original teacher who died tragically in an accident in 1979. The continuing vitality of the series is a tribute to his vision.

Roger Lockyer

The General Editor

Roger Lockyer, Emeritus Reader in History at the University of London, is the author of a number of books on Tudor and Stuart history including *Buckingham*, a political biography of George Villiers, and *The Early Stuarts: A Political History of England 1603–1642*. He has also written two widely used general surveys – *Tudor and Stuart Britain* and *Habsburg and Bourbon Europe*.

Note on the system of references

A bold number in round brackets (5) in the text refers the reader to the corresponding entry in the Bibliography section at the end of the book. A bold number in square brackets, preceded by 'doc.' [doc. 6], refers the reader to the corresponding item in the section of Documents, which follows the main text. Items followed by an asterisk * the first time they appear in a paragraph are explained in the Glossary.

Acknowledgements

The publishers are grateful to Armand Colin for permission to reproduce a table from A. Guéry, *Les finances de la monarchie française sous l'ancien régime*, Annales, ESC.

The cover: Josef Werner: *The Triumph of Louix XIV*, 1664, Château de Versailles (© Photo R.M.N., Paris).

For my parents

Introduction

By its grandeur and splendour, the monarchy of Louis XIV has for three centuries now captured our attention. At great cost to the people of France, admittedly, the King and his ministers transformed the image of kingship in Europe and succeeded in identifying Louis XIV with monarchy itself. The long reign witnessed the construction of Europe's most immense royal palace, at Versailles, royal patronage of the arts on a grand scale, attempts at the reform of taxation and the laws, and the emergence of France as the greatest single state in Europe, able to fight numerous campaigns against its neighbours. Louis XIV, the 'Sun King', easily eclipsed his fellow monarchs and dazzled contemporaries and historians alike.

Nevertheless, Louis' reign has always been the focal point for debate. Even in his own time he was attacked as a tyrant, and it was Voltaire's *Age of Louis XIV* (45) that first defended him in a work of serious scholarship. Later, Lemontey (46), Tocqueville and their followers saw him as the architect of the centralised state. For many years now an orthodox view of Louis XIV has prevailed, bolstered by the constant republication of works of hagiography and outdated scholarship. They tend to focus too much on the King himself, on his court, ministers and mistresses, and accept at face value the image projected in documents by royal propaganda. Nevertheless, in the last generation a tremendous amount of new research has been published, and it is now possible to see behind the façade of King, state and society, and present a very different picture. This short reappraisal aims to combine a presentation of the basic information with an introduction to the debates.

Such a prominent historical figure has clearly benefited from many generations of research, and most of the basic information has been available to us for many years. The nineteenth century saw the publication of many volumes of administrative correspondence, which remain important sources (1–3). However, new currents in historiography have put the accent not so much on the political events of the period, about which we already knew a great deal, but on their context. We now understand so much better than before the structures of politics, the fabric of social and political life, the way people then saw the world, their sets of values and the limits of their perceptions. Instead of seeing the seventeenth century through the eyes of the nineteenth-century historians, who focused on the 'absolutism' of the state and its bureaucracy, we can now try to understand the system of the court, and the networks of patronage and clientage that spilled over into every area of life and which were a condition for political order. All the recent work on the details of foreign policy and the curious and fascinating world of financiers has done far more than fill out a few aspects. Taken together, these studies have led to major shifts in perspective and fundamental changes in interpretation. We can now put together a much more sensitive and convincing picture.

Since the nineteenth century, many historians have suggested that Louis' reign saw a 'triumph of absolutism'. This involved the consolidation of royal power, administrative reforms and centralisation, and the curtailment of provincial and urban liberties. In the present state of studies, it hardly seems possible to go on defending such a view. By the 1980s few French or English scholarly books were even paying lip-service to the old theory, and it has become usual, in the most astute works of interpretation, to put the accent upon the survival of various aspects of 'bastard feudalism' throughout the reign and into the eighteenth century. There were slow transformations and successes, of course, and royal power was certainly made more effective in some areas, but the victory was partial and often temporary. We need to define our terms very carefully if we are to use words like 'absolute' to describe royal power *in practice* rather than its *theoretical* basis (**38**, **44**, chs. 1,2 and 4).

One of the main developments of recent years has been to situate politics inside the contemporary value-system and to show that politics and society were closely linked. It is now generally accepted that the French state was in itself something of a compromise, for the social elites were partners – and often reluctant ones – of the royal government. This compromise was taking on a different shape from the 1630s, and its nature became clearer after the end of the *Frondes** in the 1650s. As we shall see, it involved an increase of royal power not so much *against* the local elites as *with their help*. Both sides benefited from the re-establishment of order. From this compromise, the King got his way most of the time, usually on condition of being sensitive to vested interests; the elites, benefiting from stability, were happy to cooperate with a regime that confirmed their privileges and accorded them patronage and social superiority. Much of the bargain rested on the system of privilege* and the profitable opportunities provided by the financial system (**140**, **64**, **37**).

In order to achieve their aims, the King and his ministers would have liked to impose the power of the state in a more systematic fashion. The early years were decades of reform, but the primacy of foreign policy in the tasks of a ruler led to the disruption of reform by the financial necessities of war. Most of the reforms were either abandoned or simply ignored, while the elite benefited from a sort of tacit bargain with the monarchy. Thus, by the end of the reign, the socio-political system which had been modified in an *ad hoc* fashion was even more entrenched, and this system was full of contradictions and impediments to royal power.

Historians used to believe that Louis and his ministers followed grand designs, especially in foreign policy. From the 1660s onwards, it was argued, France was aiming at 'natural frontiers', or at the Spanish succession. Unfortunately, the history of foreign-policy decisions, set in their proper context of broad principles, factional struggles, misjudgements and the inevitable misreadings of the situation, does not confirm this. On the contrary, if any generalisation is true, it is that the conduct of foreign affairs was largely *ad hoc*, sometimes emotional and often counterproductive. It is a sad paradox that the period of the most effective foreign policy by Louis XIV was during his later years, when the follies of his youth had alienated most of Europe from France, and all his skill was needed to avert disaster. The so-called 'successful' period up to the 1680s, although it led to a rounding out of French frontiers, actually created deep suspicion of France's intentions and set the scene for the great European coalitions against France in the Nine Years War (1688–97) and the War of the Spanish Succession (1702–13).

The modern interpretation of Louis' reign is more complex, less easy to categorise, than the other version. If Louis is to be set in his time, this means piecing together the specific relationships of an array of unfamiliar factors – unfamiliar because they have often been ignored in the standard works. This itself poses problems of exposition, as many events were the product of a range of conditions. For example, foreign policy should not be seen in isolation. For Louis himself, foreign policy was undoubtedly the most important concern, but even he was bound by the resources that he could mobilise. Some decisions must therefore be explained in the context of internal politics, be it the dominance of one faction or the influence of religious ideology, or the financial situation. Similarly, internal policy, by temporarily putting the royal finances on a sounder basis, made possible a grander foreign policy from the 1660s to the 1680s. Yet this had the paradoxical effect of undermining the finances and forcing ministers back to the bad old ways. At times the impression is not of progress but of circularity. The reign was long, and the several factors interrelate in different ways at different times. The reader might care to bear these connections in mind when reading the separate chapters of this book.

If domestic considerations affected foreign policy, the reverse is also true. The monarchy was unable to escape from a certain tutelage to the groups controlling the hard cash needed for the wars, and had to confirm those aspects of the social order, such as privilege*, which it was in its long-term interests to attack. Even so, the crown could not entirely avoid opposition on religious and political grounds, particularly at the end of the reign. In short, for the modern historian, the reign of Louis XIV is coming to look more like a successful balancing act against a backdrop of grandeur than a real triumph of the state. It is right to insist on the great achievements of Louis, taken in their seventeenth-century context, for he was indeed the very incarnation of old regime monarchy. But this *ancien régime** monarchy was severely limited by the social, economic, geographical and political realities of the day.

Part One: The Background

1   Historical Background

The political situation in 1661

In 1661, France had just emerged from twenty-five years of foreign war against the Habsburgs of the Spanish and Austrian empires. 'Disorder reigned everywhere,' wrote Louis at this time – disorder in the court, in finance, in the church, in the nobility and in the administration of justice (**7**). Since 1624, by a policy of subsidies, and from 1635 by force of arms, French foreign policy had aimed at breaking the potential stranglehold on France occasioned by the rise of Spanish power and Spain's possession of territories around the borders, a situation made all the more dangerous by the family alliance between Philip IV and his Habsburg relatives, the Holy Roman Emperors. By a supreme effort that bore down heavily on all classes of society, but especially on the people, France had managed to raise armies which held off the foe and finally, as much by exhausting the resources of the others as by inflicting some important military defeats, led to peace treaties. It had been a close-run thing, as no early modern state had the financial system to support a war of such length with such large armies, and internal revolts were frequent. Even after having resorted to all possible expedients to raise funds, both Spain and France were bankrupt in 1648 – but France slightly less so than its rival (**134**, **138**).

The Peace of Westphalia in 1648 put an end to the Thirty Years War. These treaties formed the fundamental reference point of foreign policies for the next few generations, and saw the emergence of new powers: Sweden, the Dutch Republic and Austria. The Emperor had been forced to abandon his Spanish ally, and make a separate peace, promising not to intervene in the fight over the Spanish Netherlands that Mazarin wished to annex, but Spain continued to fight on. By these treaties France emerged as the first power in Europe. Spanish encirclement was broken and French borders were extended to the Pyrenees, and territorial gains were made on the eastern frontiers. Ten Alsacian towns passed to France and its sovereignty was recognised over the three key fortress towns of Metz, Toul and Verdun. On the one hand these gains strengthened France's borders, and on the other they were potential bridgeheads for the eventual acquisition of Spanish Franche-Comté and imperial Alsace. They also effectively isolated the Spanish Netherlands. The conditions of authority over the transferred territories were left vague by the treaty makers, as each side secretly hoped either to build on, or to reverse the decisions. Not until November 1659 was peace made between France and Spain. In that year, Spain ceded mainly territory on the French side of the Pyrenees, most notably Roussillon, and agreed to the marriage of the Infanta Maria Theresa to Louis XIV (144).

The 'disorder' of which Louis spoke had been greatly increased by the wars, but it was also a deeply rooted part of the French social and political system. The French state was in fact a collection of diverse provinces, regions and towns, which had been brought together by the dynastic and military policies of the monarchs over several centuries. The most recent acquisitions, like Burgundy, Brittany, Provence, and now Roussillon and Artois, all on the periphery, retained their provincial liberties*, their customary law codes and their institutions, usually including provincial estates. For a long time, so too did many of the older areas of France, like Normandy, Languedoc and Guyenne. Even the historically central areas, such as the Ile de France, the Orléanais, Berry, Touraine, all retained some elements of their liberties, with differing customary law codes, weights and measures, not to mention the numerous towns with tax exemptions – although as *pays d'élections** they were under much tighter royal control than the *pays d'états**. To Louis, this lack of uniformity was a fact of life, but it was nevertheless undesirable; it was an affront to classical or rational notions of the right ordering of a society that was a reflection of a divine hierarchy, headed by a respected monarch.

But there were real disorders too, as various elements in society protested against the changes in the form of government and taxation that had been imposed, supposedly temporarily, on the nation. They had begun in 1630, when higher taxation combined with plague to produce misery and protest. Throughout the 1630s and 1640s popular revolts, both rural and urban, had erupted. They were usually sparked off either by the imposition of a new tax or by the presence of fiscal agents of the royal government, and the urban elites and local nobility often connived with the rebels for a while, until it became too dangerous. Mazarin's failure to make peace with Spain in 1648, the desire to defend local and corporate privileges* against the blackmailing and divisive fiscal expedients of the monarchy, all combined with the constitutional weakness of the Regency (1643–51) and the resurgence of the political ambitions of several *grands*, to lead to the civil wars from 1648 to 1653, known as the *Frondes** (**42, 43, 127, 130**).

The *Frondes** broke out in 1649 and continued intermittently until 1653, when weariness and royal victories put an end to them. Historians now tend to regard the *Frondeurs* as an improbable combination of particularist forces with no constructive common aims, but they brought France to within an ace of collapse. The *Frondes* undoubtedly contributed to that seventeenth-century sense of living on the brink of a precipice, over a pit of disorder, which produced such a strong reaction both in royal policy and the arts. Louis himself and his ministers learned many lessons about France and the limits of royal power, and whilst they were wary of renewed opposition they were determined to make a repetition impossible.

The financial collapse brought about by the *Frondes** was only surmounted by a generous policy towards the financiers in the 1650s. Credit was re-established with difficulty by Fouquet, the superintendant of finances, and the campaigns against Spain were paid for by advances from financiers, higher taxes and more pressure on the privileged groups – in short, by a return to the policies of the 1640s. The necessary but unpopular *traitants** or *partisans** – men who had bought the right to collect certain dues and levies in return for advance payment – once again set no bounds to their rapacity. Forced loans, wine taxes and the diversion of the municipal taxes to the treasury produced numerous urban riots in the late 1650s. They were particularly serious in Aix-en-Provence and Marseille, where royal authority was openly flouted. Rural revolts occurred also, in the Sologne and in the south-west, sparked by rumours of tax reductions. In 1657, 1658 and 1659 there were assemblies of nobles, beginning in Normandy, quickly followed in other provinces, hoping to bring about a meeting of the Estates General. The outbreaks of disorder in 1659 were brutally crushed, in a portent of things to come, as the monarchy benefited from peace with Spain. Only with peace could there be a return to order and a true restoration of monarchical authority. This was to be the programme for the first decade of the personal rule of Louis XIV. Even so, significant limits to royal power were to remain throughout the reign, and only by looking more closely at the economy and society can we understand them.

Economy and society

The French economy and society in the middle years of the seventeenth century shaped and limited the political possibilities. The
essential and underlying features of early modern France included
factors such as population, agriculture and manufactures, the use
and circulation of money, the patterns of landholdings, the various
social groups, the local, provincial and royal administration, the
nature of officeholding, and social mobility. All these aspects went
to make up a society that was very set in its ways and remarkably
resistant to the imposition of change by the King and his ministers.
Indeed, rather than analysing how royal policy moulded society to
its will, it makes better historical sense to try to understand how
society framed, conditioned or modelled the French monarchical
state.

It is impossible to give a precise figure for the population of
France in Louis XIV's reign. Births, marriages and deaths were
somewhat haphazardly recorded by parish priests during this
period, and other evidence, such as taxation rolls, tends to be
difficult to use because the registers were not designed to record
all the population – only the taxable section, and even then only
the heads of families. Recent research into the history of the
population has produced the following generalisations: in 1600
there were about 16 million inhabitants of France, in 1700 about
19,300,000, give or take 10 per cent as a margin for error. The
birth-rate could fluctuate wildly according to material conditions.
Women would have about one child every two-and-a-half years
after marriage, and the average number of births per family was
somewhere between four and five. The popular image today is of
large families, but while it is true that the household might include
other relations sometimes, as well as servants, the nuclear family
was actually the norm in many regions.

The number of children per marriage was so few because
women married late, and because one or other parent would
perhaps die, with an early death around the age of forty being
quite usual. Late marriage was normally a result of poor couples
waiting until they could save up or inherit enough to establish
themselves, in an age when there was competition for land to cultivate. Women tended to get married in their mid-twenties, the men
a little later, unless a dearth of bread or a plague had reduced the
local population and left land in the hands of the younger generation. In fact, for this reason, after each calamity the population

would quickly regain its former level, with the result that France had a young and hard-working population. Only the healthy survived, and about half of those born died before reaching their twenties. Parish records show few illegitimate babies, and demographers have tended to speculate that rural morality was strict or, conversely, that marriage was postponed until motherhood approached, or, quite simply, that illegitimacy was concealed (**114, 107**)!

The vast majority of this population whose lives were so precarious lived in the countryside. They might be familiar with the small market towns, of at most a few thousand inhabitants, but large towns were rare. In the countryside, taking the *élection** of Beauvais as an example, 22 per cent of land was owned by the church, 22 per cent by the nobility, 13 per cent by the bourgeoisie* and 43 per cent by the peasantry. Of course, most of the clergy, nobility and bourgeoisie rented out their landed estates to tenant farmers who not only organised the cultivation of this land but also saw to the enforcement and collection of the seigneurial* dues which were attached to the land. There would be perhaps one such *fermier** in every parish. Next down the social scale came the substantial peasant, known as a *laboureur*, who owned a horse and plough. For such families, Pierre Goubert cites figures of 3 in 86 households in one village, 1 in 46 in another and 6 out of 70 in a third (**110**).

Finally came the mass of peasants who owned less than 5 acres of land. Since it took about 25 acres to support a family, or 8 or 9 if one specialised in vines instead of grain, it is clear that most peasants in this class had to supplement their income by hiring themselves out as day labourers and by practising some home craft during the periods of agricultural inactivity. In many areas this extra work took the form of producing poor-quality cloth, especially in the Beauvais region, near Amiens, and in Languedoc. During the seventeenth century there was in the north-east and south-west of France a tendency for estates to get bigger as the small peasant proprietors fell into debt and sold their plots of land; consequently, the numbers of landless labourers increased (**108, 111, 116**).

Until the 1630s in the north and the 1670s in the south, agricultural production was on the increase, and bread prices were lowish; but by the early years of the personal rule of Louis XIV the economic trends had changed everywhere. Now the situation markedly worsened, production fell and food prices increased, and these conditions were to last until the end of the reign. 'By

1700 in Burgundy the rural communities were crippled by
taxation, whole communities were in debt and harvests had
worsened. Small farmers tended to fail in the Beauvaisie, and in
Provence there was soil erosion due to excessive land clear-
ance'(**112,** p. 165). The land provided far less profit for the
landowners, as peasant cultivators fell into debt, arrears piled up
and there was no one to take on new tenancies. Rents fell and so
therefore did landed revenue. Naturally, the landlords shortened
their leases and tried to have payment in money instead of in kind,
but even these strategies were not enough to stop profits declining.
The English and Dutch solution of new agricultural techniques
was beyond the capacity of French society. Thus, the years of Louis
XIV were years of growing agricultural crisis, exacerbated in the
early 1660s and 1690s by bad harvests. This economic background
profoundly conditioned and limited the development of the
monarchy (**107, 108**).

Vagrancy was a major and endemic problem, and numbers
increased in times of bad harvests. Vagrants would flock to the
towns for assistance, only to be put on the road back to their parish
of origin for fear of straining urban resources. It has been said that
in seventeenth-century France 75 per cent of the peasantry cultivated insufficient land for what are today considered the barest
essentials of human existence. These conditions remained the
same until after the 1720s (**116**). Their consequence was that
neither the seigneur* nor the King could increase their share of
the peasants' produce very much without forcing the poor family
under. So the limits of royal taxation were set by the agrarian structures, and the best prospects for increasing royal revenue lay in
taxing hitherto exempt groups and by encouraging the growth of
commercial wealth which was more easily taxable. Ministers such
as Colbert did not fail to draw these conclusions.

Production in the towns was almost entirely artisanal, taking
place in small workshops run by masters employing two or three
journeymen and apprentices. Workshops from the same trades
tended to be grouped together in the same street or quarter,
which made for close-knit communities, resistant to outside interference. In the modern sense of the word, there was no industry in
France at this time. Gaston Zeller writes: 'The importance of rural
trades in France in this period cannot be over-emphasised. Most
industrial work had rural roots and the majority of those who were
engaged in it were agricultural labourers' (**115,** p. 143). Again, to
cite Jean Meuvret, one of the great economic historians: 'Most

artisans did not form a class separate from the peasants. They generally combined both activities' (**115,** p. 142). If textiles were primarily a rural industry, metal and glassworks were even more exclusively rural. There were no factories to speak of, only forty-eight existed in France in 1610, and probably fewer thereafter. Colbert was to add to their number, but they were concentrations of labour under one roof rather than factories in our modern and technological sense, and few survived for long. For the most part they owed their existence not to the spirit of capitalism but to royal initiatives, of which there were to be more in the 1660s. In setting up and encouraging these 'manufactures' the government hoped to produce in France the high-quality goods such as silk which, if imported from abroad, drained capital and specie from the realm.

Another feature of the French economy was a constant worry for Colbert and his successors: the nature of trade and the dearth of monetary circulation. The saleable commodities exported by France were wheat, grain, wine, spirits, salt and cloth. The return for the exports might be other goods or gold and silver coin, but since peasants did not use coins of large denomination and merchants kept no cash reserves in quantity, relatively few coins were minted. Most trade was paid for by bills of exchange and letters of credit which circulated in the locality between merchants [**doc. 19**]. Peasants only patronised local artisans, and purchases were made by exchanges or with copper coins worth actually less than their face value. In the countryside, therefore, a barter economy prevailed. It was probably only when the countryfolk took their harvest to market, in the autumn, that they received some of the small-denomination silver coins, which they could use to pay the tax collector and seigneur*. The lack of gold and silver coinage was a European phenomenon in this period, and not only did it have a restrictive effect on trade but it also made it more difficult to find the hard cash to pay for military supplies and for the armies. Seen in this light, policies that aimed at keeping the maximum of specie in the realm, and which attempted to attract more in, were not so irrational. Such policies were to be at the root of Colbert's trade wars (**118**).

The medieval division of French society into three orders or estates still corresponded to social values. As the First Estate, the clergy was a separate order which claimed jurisdiction over its own affairs and exemptions from taxation; if many clerics felt more French (Gallican) in their allegiance than Roman, some were not above playing off the Pope against the King in matters of royal control or doctrine, and the whole order would readily combine to defend its financial independence by appealing, over the King's head, to the Pontiff. In cases of conflict all the old arguments about being those who prayed for society – and society did remain profoundly religious in its outlook – would be trotted out to justify clerical immunity. It was the same with the nobility, which comprised the Second Estate. In spite of debates on the nature of nobility, and changes in the composition of the army, the power-fully dominant view was still that nobles were privileged because they fought to defend the commonwealth, and because they were particularly virtuous (**191**). Thus they should not be made to pay direct taxation of the same nature as commoners, and should be distinguished from all others in society by their dress and lifestyle, both of which should reflect their rank. Although many nobles were of recent origin, having acquired their titles by office or by purchase, they all adopted and shared the same values and felt that they belonged to an order with an honourable thousand-year history. These values were accepted by King, courtiers, ministers and society at large, and the ideology of nobility therefore remained the pre-eminent set of values. Thus, even though the nobility ranged from the poor *hobereau* reduced to cultivating his own land to the immensely wealthy duke and peer at court, the group conserved its extensive privileges (**109**).

From the Third Estate, the bourgeoisie* is the most difficult group to define precisely, because it was made up of so many different elements. 'Bourgeois' had originally meant an inhabitant of a town, but the predominant meaning was now that of a person at the top of the urban hierarchy enjoying rights and exemptions, who did not engage in productive labour but rather lived off his investments. Royal officeholding was the principal channel of social mobility, as offices combined investment with social prestige (**98**). Their attraction is obvious, because the upper ranks in the system of venal offices* conferred nobility. In many cases the bourgeois might therefore be an officeholder in the judiciary or the financial administration, in one of the royal courts perhaps, or as a member of the town council, and little distinguished him from a noble except the fact that he had not yet acquired a recognised title of nobility. (He would almost certainly have purchased a seigneurie* and thereby picked up an aristocratic sounding 'de' before the name of his landed estate.) Many towns were dominated by such men, while others contained an influential mercantile bourgeoisie engaged in wholesale trade and perhaps international commerce, as in Marseille, Brest, Nantes, La Rochelle, Bordeaux, Strasbourg, or Lyon. Also members of the Third Estate were the smaller traders, masters and producers who made up the bulk of the order. Yet, these lesser families counted for little in the social hierarchy in spite of their numbers and economic importance, and they had few privileges*.

In the village, the most obvious face of privilege* was the seigneurial* system. The lord, without having the use of the land, owned an assortment of burdensome rights over it. These would be the *champart** (about 10 per cent of the crop levied in kind), quit-rents, hunting rights, the obligation to use the seigneurial mill and press, and the valuable privilege of rendering justice – and thus of protecting and enforcing his own claims. Non-nobles could own seigneurial rights, on payment of the 'franc-fief', and the bourgeoisie* frequently did so, especially around the towns. Not only was the investment in land attractive, but the rights that went with landownership made one appear noble – and this was the height of bourgeois aspirations.

Privileges* were a fundamental fact of life in seventeenth-century France. They were recognised in law and by generations of traditional practice. The notion of privilege itself was unassailable, and in the eyes of society the monarchy existed to defend privilege, as this was a part of its obligation to uphold good order in the state. However, although the crown could not attack the principle of privilege, it could withdraw specific liberties* or rights as a punishment for disobedience. Towns or provinces that revolted might lose their privileges, as did Marseille in 1660, and the Boulonnais in 1662 [**docs 15** and **16**]. Usually the loss of privileges was temporary: the concept could be exploited as a technique of government, by playing on the desire for privilege to secure obedience – as with the confirmation of rights at the end of every session of provincial estates. Offices sold with privileges were more attractive to the purchaser, and therefore brought in more to the royal treasury. Similarly, letters patent recognising noble rank, and thereby opening the way to the enjoyment of further privileges, could be sold for a nice profit. All these examples demonstrate that the monarchy had to act in a manner that conformed to the prevailing law and conventions. The need for the King to act in accordance with law, even with respect to what were from his point of view onerous and positively undesirable rights and exemptions, also created a moral barrier to the enlargement of royal power. The exploitation for financial gain of a principle so opposed to good organisation – and, indeed, to the long-term interest of the crown – is one of the many paradoxes of Louis XIV's regime.

The social politics of royal finance

Finance was one of the central preoccupations of the government. Wars, the royal household and prestige projects needed large revenues to cover their costs. The only assured revenue came from the royal domain, the *taille** (a hearth tax which had become permanent during the Hundred Years War), and various excise taxes. However, expansion of the royal revenue was not easy. Both by its attitudes and its structures society was resistant to demands for increased taxes (**44**, ch. 10). The belief that the King should live off his own income from the royal domain remained a strong barrier, as did the idea that extra taxation in times of trouble was a temporary resource that should not be continued in peacetime. The church believed itself immune from direct taxation by virtue of its spiritual role, and was only prepared to grant a 'free gift' at its quinquennial Assembly. Similarly, the provinces with estates defended their liberties* and the principle that taxation could only be granted after deliberation, which implied a tacit or explicit bargain over the redress of grievances [**doc. 28**]. Naturally, they paid less than their fair proportion of the national burden.

To get money, the ministers exploited the already existing sources, but also had constant recourse to men who offered new ideas for increasing royal revenue by new indirect taxes. Thus a system had grown up in which the necessary regular income, which greatly exceeded that provided by the domain and the *taille**, was brought up to the necessary level by a variety of prerogative levies, and by taxes, known as *traités**, levied indirectly on the sale or transport of goods. After forty years of involvement in foreign war, the system was confusing (even to contemporaries!), and exploited all manner of expedients, themselves stretched beyond their limits. Not only was it a complicated system, but it was also a system full of abuses (**142**), whose study leads to surprising conclusions about the nature of the monarchy.

Overall, direct taxation seems to have amounted to between 5 and 10 per cent of a peasant's production in most years – much lower than today, therefore – but there were wide variations both in time and space. The incidence of the *taille** often bore no relationship to the revenue of a village, and a community earning little might be taxed as much as one that was much more prosperous, even in the same neighbourhood. Between regions the difference could be great, as the *pays d'états** paid on average far less to the crown than the *pays d'élections** (although in Brittany the peasants paid a heavy burden of tax both to their seigneurs* and to the provincial estates). In times of dearth or disease, or foreign wars – all periods when trade tended to contract and income fall – the taxes became proportionally heavier. Although the average percentage was not high, they were added to seigneurial dues and the clerical tithe. The fact that taxes might double even in hard times, as the *taille* did from 1701 to 1709 (because sales taxes were bringing in less), could help to explain the periods of fiscal revolt and disturbances. Royal taxes seem to have been thought less acceptable than the seigneurial dues that were at least hallowed by long custom. Consequently, popular revolts tended to focus their hostility on royal tax collectors rather than seigneurs*, although here again Brittany is an exception (**127–9**).

As we have seen, there were basically four means available to the state for acquiring funds. The first was the revenue from the leasing of the royal domain; the second, the direct tax called the *taille**, a hearth tax which fell mainly on the peasants, the third was a host of indirect taxes known as the *aides**, *traités** and *gabelles**, the latter being an iniquitous tax on salt; and the fourth source was loans. Leaving aside some nuances, the first three were collected either by agents employed directly by the crown (and who held offices), or by private companies who, in return for collecting the tax, were allowed to keep the difference between what they contracted to pay the King and what they actually collected. This private system, known as tax farming, was widespread in seventeenth- and eighteenth-century Europe (**137**).

Sale of office itself was a part of the financial system. It had become a way of raising loans from the richer sections of bourgeois society in return for prestige and a very small *gage*, or interest payment. In fact, when the crown first alienated a royal office the sum paid might be tens of thousands of *livres**, but once alienated the office would be resold privately and the only royal revenue was from the *annuel**, a tax which the King levied in return for allowing officeholders to pass on their offices to their heirs. This situation explains the attraction to the government of creations of new offices, useful or not, and the doubling up of existing offices to be exercised alternately, all for a quick profit. Since many offices conferred nobility, venality of office* was also a vital part of the patterns of social mobility, associating social power with office, and wealth with exemption from direct taxation. Forced loans were an expedient that attempted to tap the rich, who enjoyed exemptions from direct taxes because of their privileges of rank and office.

The greater part of revenue came from 'extraordinary affairs', such as sale of office, but more importantly from loans of all sorts. The needs of war having far outstripped the regular income from the royal domain and the *taille**, the King was forced to have greater recourse to borrowed money. A glance at a table of royal revenue in the second half of the century reveals that the greatest proportion of expenditure was financed by indirect taxes and loans(**135**). According to recent research, during the first half of the century a chaotic system of loan finance had grown up. This system operated through the financiers, who usually used straw men for their contracts and drew their funds not so much from personal wealth as from rich aristocrats, courtiers and merchants. The financiers would advance the hard-pressed crown money in return for interest. Since these rates of interest were higher than the monarchy's own laws permitted, the ministers themselves encouraged concealment of the deals, as well as fraudulent accounting. They had no choice if they were to get the money, but they also took advantage of the possibilities this situation created for building up a personal clientele on the strength of the illicit profits. By the 1660s most of the ordinary royal revenue was mortgaged to pay for loans at an exorbitant rate of interest, and contracts were being made for advances to be recouped by the financiers who in effect proposed and bought the right to collect specified taxes. In 1661, according to Colbert's figures, the monarchy was 451 million *livres** in debt – and this was more than five years' ordinary revenue (**138–40**).

Of course, everybody hated the financiers, as is shown by contemporary songs, pamphlets and plays (Dancourt, *Les Agioteurs*; Le Sage, *Turcaret*), but they were none the less necessary. Popular feeling against their rapacity was so strong that King and ministers pretended to share the hatred, all the while knowing that to attack the financiers was to attack their own relatives and courtiers who put up the money which the financiers used. Nevertheless, the hatred could be exploited (as in 1661) to renege on debts and put some financiers on trial for fraud – in order to fine them as a way of cancelling more debts! These procedures profoundly marked the monarchy and may seem incredible to the modern observer, but they are well attested. We shall see how Colbert and Louis XIV exploited these hatreds for their own purposes, and how the financiers operated during Louis' later period (**140**).

For the monarchy, this financial system was to have serious consequences. The weight of taxes and the corruption associated with their levy produced grinding poverty for the peasants, who were scraping a living on a subsistence level. Moreover, money was not invested in agricultural improvements and commerce by those who could have afforded it. Instead, it was drained off into prestigious offices and state finances. The fiscal pressure on all classes of society, even on the supposedly exempt (for the government's practice of defaulting on loans and reducing interest rates on its debts were a sort of tax on the rich) produced discontent and revolt. Louis XIV's comment about the potential for disorder in France in 1661 was all too soundly based.

Justice and administration

Although the word 'bureaucracy' is often used for the royal administration, it can give a misleading impression of systematic paperwork, of a genuine hierarchy of command in offices and of governmental efficiency. In practice, all of these aspects were greatly deficient and sometimes non-existent. The failure lay less in the paperwork, for many of the ministers and officials were indefatigable scribblers, than in the hierarchy. Since offices were purchased and their incumbents were virtually irremovable, officials were free to give their loyalty to those best able to further their interests. In a general sense this was to the King, but he was far away, and if his representative, the governor, was in conflict with another body representing him, for example the parlement*, it was up to each man to decide for himself where his interests lay. By the mid-seventeenth century clientage or *fidélité* was far less rigid than in medieval times. Indeed, a client would often abandon a patron who failed to deliver the expected favours. Officials were enmeshed in networks of patronage and clientage, without which there was no social mobility, no promotion and little status, and through which conflicts were expressed. In each town or parlement, a faction would exist which supported the governor, and one which upheld the independence of the institution against him. The basis for such conflicts continued to exist well after the end of the *Frondes** (**98–102**).

French society was very legalistic, and a hierarchy of law courts existed, with a system of appeals to higher jurisdictions. The seigneurial* courts held sway in the villages of France, but royal justice began in the towns where bailiwick* courts existed, above which were the important parlements*, which were not only courts of appeal but also had extensive administrative competence. The most important parlement was that of the Paris region, which in terms of jurisdiction meant about a third of France. Above the parlements, but interfering little in ordinary matters, was the royal council of state staffed by masters of requests*. Courts of accounts existed too in many provinces. Each court was so jealous of its jurisdiction and prerogatives that conflicts were normal and efficiency was greatly reduced, while costs for the litigant naturally increased with each appeal. Small wonder that many cases dragged on for years. The fact that the principle of the judicial system was not punishment but redress, conciliation and making amends, encouraged determined parties in the belief that possession was nine-tenths of the law. We still know far too little about the courts in this period, as research has focused on the central government (**67**).

If we accept that the courts were relatively independent bodies even though they dealt with most of what we would today call administration – they called it *police** – the only elements of a strict bureaucracy lay in the thirty or so intendants*. These were masters of requests* in the King's council who were sent on mission into the provinces or the army, to observe and interfere where necessary, especially in financial matters. They were emissaries of the royal council and thus had considerable judicial authority, and could even alter tax assessments at will (**86**). Their special powers were offensive to existing officeholders and influential tax-evaders, and they were widely disliked, to the extent that conflicts were numerous [**docs 20–5**]. Colbert's solution to this problem was to confine them more closely to specific issues described in their letters of commission. The ministers' chief problem in governing was lack of information, and one of the intendants' main tasks was to observe and report back [**doc. 12**]. However, as the only royal agents directly responsible to the council, with revocable commissions (and therefore more reliable), they were employed so frequently that they soon became a permanent feature of the administration. Moreover, they began to employ sub-delegates to help them, which led to the development of a (limited) new bureaucracy alongside the traditional administration. But the intendants should not be characterised as a homogenous group, nor as characteristic of royal government under Louis XIV. Great as their efforts were, their quality varied and there were only twenty-three in 1679, and thirty at the end of the reign (**88**). They did not eclipse the governors (who have hardly been studied at all), because the governors developed their own role as patronage-brokers between the provinces and the court, particularly where the provincial estates were concerned. As for routine administrative matters, governors were often happy to leave these to the intendants.

How does all this change our picture of the 'absolute' monarchy at the beginning of the personal rule? Clearly, it gives us a radically different one in terms of the actual and potential power of the monarchy. Instead of ruling France with an iron hand, we see the monarchy as the prisoner of a system virtually incapable of reform because credit would dry up – a monarchy based on, or rather embedded in, the very social structure it was once thought to have dominated. Essential to this new view is the realisation that in 1661 the monarchy lacked the means to exercise its power effectively. The provinces were unwilling to give up their particular liberties for the common good, and were entrenched behind legal barriers to royal power which the crown was unwilling as well as unable to breach. The machinery or structure of government itself was a system unresponsive to pressure, even from the King and his ministers, because it was based ultimately on the court, and the court was a place of faction, an arena well-suited to the self-preserving tactics of the aristocratic elite (**68–70**). Louis had only limited room for manoeuvre, since the court was the keystone in the whole edifice of patronage and clientage (**20**, ch. 3). The continued importance of the nobility both at court and in the financial operations of the royal government, now generally accepted by scholars, runs counter to the myth of a new monarchy allied with a rising bourgeoisie*, working together against the nobility (e.g.: **44,** ch. 3, and **59**). The monarchy of Louis XIV was profoundly aristocratic. It is with this in mind that we must now move on to study the activities of the King and his ministers.

Part Two: Analysis

2 King, Court and Ministers

If Louis had genius, it lay in the art of kingship. For contemporaries he was the incarnation of monarchy in its grandeur and its splendour. But grandeur and splendour are images, one might almost say illusions, not necessarily based on lasting practical achievements in politics. Perhaps historians have been wrong to see Louis as a man who aimed at a transformation of the Renaissance monarchy into a modern state. Elements of this transformation may have been the result of his ministers' practical policies, but it is hard to argue that such a vision existed and that it was his intention. It seems evident in his *Mémoires* (**7**) and from studies of the practice of his government that Louis well understood the traditional limitations on monarchical activity. He had been brought up to believe that he was a monarch by divine right, which implied that he owed his sovereignty to God, not to the people. This sovereignty was therefore not shared with any other body, which made it 'absolute', or entire and freed from restraint. But there were moral and practical restraints, in the form of his Christian duties and the existing laws, privileges* and institutions of the realm. Louis never disputed this: he had a veneration for tradition and considerable respect for the established social order and its institutions – he even praised the parlements* for their historic existence in spite of their role in the *Frondes**. He was not by nature anything of a revolutionary, nor did he seek to transform the political system radically. He was very much the heir to his predecessors Henri IV and Louis XIII, who had been bringing about more or less slow and *ad hoc* changes. In a traditional and hierarchical society radical change was almost unthinkable, and Louis was a man of his age.

Thus it is in vain that historians have tried to substantiate a view of Louis that casts him in the role of a bureaucrat or an 'absolute' ruler exercising unlimited power in the modern sense. Certainly, he wanted to exercise more power than his predecessors, whose achievements had been undermined by the revolts and resistance of the preceding decades. He wanted to restore good order to his kingdom and ensure the security of the monarchy. But his chief aim was to acquire glory for himself and for his dynasty, and he needed the means to do this. Thus control of the state was a means to an end, not an end in itself. Louis proved to be prepared to sacrifice all of Colbert's painstaking financial reforms on the altar of a glorious war. Modern research has shown the administrative achievements of Louis' reign to have been relatively slight for such a long period, largely because of the compromises that had to be made. On the other hand, the recent investigation of his policies of patronage and of propaganda, both literary and artistic, and of his cultivation of the image of the perfect courtier, has revealed his true strengths. Louis was the very image of a king, and this factor, when combined with policies of order and compromise, proved to be a vital element in his power.

Louis had been brought up to kingship from birth. Both his mother and Mazarin, even while educating him, always treated him respectfully as the King and ultimate master. He was handsome, graceful and fit, keen on military training and hunting – in short, he was every inch the nobleman. His education has often been decried as insufficient, but this is an exaggeration. He was ignorant of the texts of the Humanists that most *honnêtes hommes* of his age read, but had a good grounding in geography and French history. He spoke and wrote excellent French, which was more than either his mother or Mazarin did, and could also speak Italian well and Spanish passably. He was imbued with the belief in the divine origins of royal power, and that kings were created by God to rule and protect the divinely created earthly order. His religious education was a full one that reflected the sentiments of his mother, who regarded his birth as a miracle (**41**, ch. 2). His devotion was to increase greatly under the influence of Madame de Maintenon in the 1680s. From his mother also he must have acquired the almost Spanish taste for etiquette and ceremony that were to become such features of his court and elements of his own style of personal monarchy.

It was in practical politics that Louis' education excelled, for not only did he witness at first hand the drama of the *Frondes** and their aftermath, but he also had perhaps the finest teacher of his age: Mazarin. It would be wrong to think that the *Frondes* inspired in Louis such fears that he longed for revenge, for revenge was not a sensible option in an age when monarchical power was more a question of a subtle balance of opposing forces than of a brutal destruction of opponents. The monarchy was not so strong in 1661 that it could afford to treat former enemies with contempt. Mazarin would have taught Louis to know how to be silent, how to bide his time, how to praise one person and flatter another, how to dissimulate in order to disarm his enemies, how to woo them with favours and offer a practical and honourable compromise to families of doubtful loyalty, and how to strike hard at those foolish enough to show any lack of respect for the King. The concept of *raison d'état* formed an integral part of his view of things, by which was meant that the king had a public and private duty to the state, which was greater than that which he owed as an individual, and that the interests of the state should be evaluated in the light of hard, cold reason, and not, for example, religious or personal sentiment. The seventeenth century was an age of iron, as has often been said, and the civilised veneer of the court should not lead us to ignore the brutality of politics. There is every reason to believe that Louis recognised this himself.

Perhaps Louis' greatest asset was his taste for long hours spent reading reports and attending council meetings. From the mid-1650s, the Cardinal-minister Mazarin trained him carefully in the art of government and decision-making [**doc. 2**]. Louis emerged as a somewhat hesitant, though very shrewd, young man, with a great sense of responsibility, complete faith in himself, and a dash of impetuosity. He never doubted for a second his role as a great king. 'The *métier de roi* is grand, noble, delicious.... It is by hard work that one rules, for hard work that one rules.... The function of kings consists primarily of using good sense, which always comes naturally and easily,' he was to write in his *Mémoires* (**7**). The death of Mazarin on 9 March 1661 saw Louis struck by real grief, but he was as well prepared as any king to rule. He always gloried in the profession of king, which at the age of twenty-three he had grown impatient to exercise. His contemporaries soon had occasion to express their admiration [**doc. 4**].

Louis was passionately determined to rule.

I made it a rule to work regularly twice a day for two to three hours at a time with various persons, aside from the hours that I worked alone or that I might devote to extraordinary affairs if any arose.... I commanded the four secretaries of state to sign nothing in future without discussing it with me, and the same for the superintendent of finances, and for nothing to be transacted in the finances without being registered in a little book that was to remain with me.... I announced that all requests for graces of any type had to be made directly to me, and I granted to all my subjects the privilege of appealing to me at any time.... As to the persons who were to help me in my work, I resolved above all not to have a first minister.... In order to concentrate the entire authority of a master more fully in myself,... I resolved to enter into (details) with each of the ministers when he would least expect it. (**7**, pp. 29–32)

Much to the surprise of contemporaries, Louis was to stick to these resolutions for the rest of his life.

The King governed with the aid of his ministers, his secretaries of state and some unofficial advisers. Each of the four secretaries of state busied himself with taking lesser decisions and corresponding with those in his *département*. His tasks included, in addition to, for example, responsibility for foreign affairs, the administration of a certain number of provinces. The King's formal decisions were taken in the royal council, which was divided into separate groups meeting on different days for different affairs. From the time of the death of Mazarin, Louis reduced the over-large 'secret council' to just three members, and it soon became known informally as the Council of the Three, subsequently the *Conseil d'en haut*. This was the real centre of policy-making, where all the most important decisions were taken. Here, during the first six months of the personal rule, Louis rapidly completed his apprenticeship in government. It seems that all the decisions taken were strictly in accordance with the deathbed advice of Mazarin: 'The instructions given by the dying cardinal constituted, at least in their broad lines, the political programme that Louis and his various councils, and above all that of the three, followed faithfully' (**5**: Intro., p. lxiv). This Council of Three contained the most expert of his ministers. They were Lionne, Le Tellier and Fouquet, all former clients of Mazarin, who had long served him and the crown. After the arrest of Fouquet in September the council continued to meet every morning, with Colbert replacing his rival Fouquet.

It is not clear when meetings became less frequent. In 1667, admittedly at the start of a war, the Marquis de Saint-Maurice could still note that 'The king usually holds his council meeting twice a day, with only his three ministers and sometimes the Marshal de Turenne' (**6**, p. 29). This council of state, which also dealt with all matters of foreign affairs, normally met on

Wednesdays, Thursdays, Sundays and every other Monday. Financial matters were dealt with in the Royal Council of Finances, set up on 15 September 1661, which met twice a week, but important decisions were taken in private by Louis and his finance minister (called controller-general after 1665), and then presented to the council for formal ratification. Most domestic affairs were the concern of the Council of Dispatches, which met twice weekly. This was the largest council, since it was attended by the secretaries of state, the chancellor and princes of the blood. Other councils existed at different periods; namely, a Council of Commerce from 1664 to 1676 and from 1701 onwards, and a Council for Ecclesiastical Affairs, mostly dealing with the distribution of benefices. The latter was soon composed of only the King, his confessor and the Archbishop of Paris (**60**, ch. 1; **14**). The appearance and disappearance of the Council of Commerce, the almost informal procedure of the Religious Council and the creation of a Council of Finances bear witness not so much to an administrative revolution, as some historians have argued, as to a readiness to institutionalise the *ad hoc* and to improvise in a situation that was still fluid. It is also important to remember that because the King was a judge, all these councils were judicial bodies whose decisions took the form of judgments, rather than administrative orders. The secretaries of state would subsequently see to the dispatch of letters that we would call administrative.

It was the King's custom to seek advice privately from those courtiers he respected as well as from his ministers, and then take decisions on important matters of state in his *Conseil d'en haut*. In the later part of his reign the Ducs de Chevreuse and Beauvillier both had considerable influence. He would hear all the arguments his ministers cared to put forward, express his own views, and then on almost all occasions decide according to the majority. Some contemporaries insist that he was dominated by his ministers, who played on the excessive weight of detail and obscurity of business to influence him. Historians still differ on this point, but it is clear that most of the time Louis did all he could to have enough information to make his own decisions and to encourage objectivity. It is equally clear that no single person could hope to control effectively all areas of government, and his *Mémoires* show that he was well aware of this limitation. However, it does seem that when Louis was known to have a strong preference for a course of action, his advisers were reluctant to risk their careers and family influence by openly opposing him. They would carefully calculate their interests and, if they thought it wise, shift around to his point of view. This is what happened with Colbert on the Dutch War of 1672 and with Torcy on the decision to accept the Spanish Succession in 1701– both of whom had originally adopted contrary positions (**149–51, 156**). It also seems that as the King developed his ambitions and pride in the 1670s and 1680s, he tended to choose ministers with less strong characters and more pliability, men who would play the courtier more than the adviser.

However, the original team of the 1660s and 1670s was composed of men who were tough, competent and experienced. They all worked incredibly long hours, and even their pleasures were for the most part calculated to protect and enhance their position. Of the three, Hugues de Lionne (1611–71) was probably the most intelligent. He was a minister without a specific department. Nevertheless, it was he who directed foreign policy, having been Mazarin's confidant and second in these matters. He had acquired a wealth of experience on missions and at conferences and was 'the most able and the most agreeable negotiator of the age, a constant source of grand policies' (**5**, Intro., p. xviii). In close association with the King he dealt with dispatches and instructions to ambassadors and usually wrote out in his own hand the replies to foreign courts. So high was he in the King's esteem that even his constant loyalty to Fouquet after his disgrace was not held against him. His influence was such that he completely eclipsed his nephew Brienne, the secretary of state who was normally responsible for foreign affairs, leaving him as merely the executor of routine dispatches and orders. It was Lionne who tried to put back together a coherent foreign policy after the War of Devolution had reduced Mazarin's policy to ruins, and who tried his best to prevent the Dutch War that Louis was so determined to have. On his death in 1671 he was succeeded by Arnauld de Pomponne (1618–99), who was also a fine diplomat but without much influence in the council (**157**). From even before that date Louis, whose warlike ambitions were encouraged by Louvois, had begun to make his own foreign policy.

Michel Le Tellier (1603–85), the war minister, had also been a client or creature of Cardinal Mazarin. Like many successful members of the *noblesse de robe**, and exactly like Colbert, Le Tellier came from a family that a hundred years before had been part of the successful commercial bourgeoisie*. In view of the myth that still prevails that Louis chose 'bourgeois' ministers, it is worth paying some attention to the rise of the Le Tellier family to the rank of robe nobility and powerful royal servant. In the 1550s the family, including cousins and nephews, was either still in trade or had purchased small judicial offices. It took three generations to complete the rise to minister. Michel II (1545–1608) was a corrector in the chamber of accounts, and through his wife who was the mistress of the Duc de Mayenne, he became intendant* of finances for the Catholic League during the Wars of Religion and made a small fortune. He bought estates and, after having been an intendant in Champagne in the 1590s, acquired an office in the chamber of accounts. His son Michel III consolidated the family position and left 84,000 *livres** in cash in 1627. The care taken not to compromise the family wealth is shown by the sending of four of the six daughters to convents to save on dowries. One of the others married Colbert de Saint-Pouange, who helped Michel IV (1603–85) to buy the office of *procureur du roi* (king's attorney) in the Châtelet, while Michel's wife was a noble chosen from a family in the financial courts, who brought with her a dowry of 103,400 *livres*, and the protection of her father's brother-in-law, the Chancellor d'Aligre. From the position of representative of the King in the principal Parisian municipal court, Michel IV moved to the office of master of requests* in 1638. The really decisive moment in his career came when he was chosen for a military and diplomatic mission to Piedmont as intendant of the army. He acquitted himself well, using his own credit to facilitate supplies – and worked with Mazarin, whose star was rising rapidly. It was Mazarin who was the main influence in having Louis XIII name him secretary of state for war in 1643. With his military reforms, he was to be the organiser of victory for the next three decades.

Like any sensible minister, Le Tellier took the opportunity of developing his own clientage network by filling posts under his control with his creatures, and he was especially influential in the armies. His utter loyalty to the King, to Anne of Austria, the Queen-Mother, and to Mazarin during the *Frondes** ensured his survival in the 1650s. He was a prudent man of sound judgement and tremendous experience, who knew how to protect his interests by marrying his children and grandchildren to court families and by increasing the family fortune with large purchases of land, including the marquisate of Louvois in 1656. In Michel Le Tellier and his son François-Michel, Marquis de Louvois, the young King was to have two of his ablest ministers (**50, 51**). From 1664, Michel shared the office of secretary of state for war with his son whom he had trained so well, and from 1675 he became chancellor, an office which he held until his death in 1685. When the somewhat brutal but largely efficient Louvois died in 1691, having also acquired in 1683 the role of superintendant of the royal buildings, the family still remained powerful through its various branches. Le Tellier's wife, who survived both husband and son, left a family fortune of over 3 million *livres** in 1696, proving that the fruits of office were rich indeed.

The superintendant of finance, Nicolas Fouquet (1615–80), was already a very wealthy man by the 1640s. His great-grandfather had been a rich merchant-draper in Angers in the 1550s, a man with aristocratic pretensions who gave his son a sound legal education and orientated him towards offices. The son soon became a counsellor in the Paris parlement* in 1578, while other branches of the family consolidated their position in the local courts and more spectacularly in Brittany. It was the Breton branch that was to step in loyally in the 1590s to protect the Parisian family from the misfortune created by the premature death of two brothers in the parlement. Such solidarity is eloquent testimony to the family strategies that played a vital role in the formation of a class of high aristocracy of the robe later in the century. The family of Fouquet, and as we shall see, that of Colbert also, behaved more like a united clan than separate households. Add to this strategy a policy of complete loyalty to the monarchy in difficult times, and you have the recipe for success under the early Bourbons (**76**). The joining of two largish fortunes by the marriage of François Fouquet and a Maupeou in 1610 brought with it the patronage of the father-in-law Gilles de Maupeou, who was one of Sully's closest collaborators in the royal finances. Becoming master of requests* in 1615, Fouquet confirmed his nobility and joined an elite group of royal agents. By the late 1620s he was a trusted client of Cardinal Richelieu. His fortune as a *rentier** prospered and the family was linked with the *Parti Dévôt**, powerful in the Counter-reformation church, and at court.

Nicolas, Louis' future minister, was a particularly brilliant young man whose father bought for him the office of master of requests* in 1635 (for 150,000 *livres**) and who married a rich heiress with a dowry of 160,000 *livres* – another marriage of fortunes, therefore. Later, in 1651, having been widowed without an heir, he made a second rich and advantageous marriage which brought him courtly and financial connections. In 1640 his father had died leaving around 800,000 *livres* and the leadership of the family. Nicolas chose to invest in land and become a grand seigneur*,

while developing a career as intendant* of the army, then intendant in Dauphiné. This part of his career was rather brief, as he
was honest enough to defend the population against the *traitants**,
and was therefore temporarily disgraced. Back in favour in 1647,
he was named intendant of Paris in the difficult year of 1648, when
the *Frondes** broke out. It was a tricky political position that he
knew how to exploit.

Subtle, diplomatic and above all loyal to Mazarin, Fouquet
played an important role in dividing the opposition during the
Frondes*. His recompense was to be appointed as one of two superintendants of finances in 1653, the youngest financial controller of
the *ancien régime**. His task was to raise funds to provide for the war
against Spain – and, incidentally, for the re-establishment of his
patron Mazarin's personal fortune. Ready at all times to use his
own credit on behalf of the monarchy, he succeeded in doing all
that was required – an almost superhuman task – and in increasing
his own fortune modestly. Naturally, he developed his own
network of financial contacts willing and able to invest in risky but
sometimes profitable royal finances, and that included many
leading courtiers. Public finances was a nasty business, and
Fouquet was no choirboy, but it does seem that the later accusations of excessive profits and corruption levelled against him by
Colbert were only as true of him as they were of Colbert himself. It
is important to understand that Fouquet's display of wealth and
conspicuous lifestyle were both part of the financial game in which
appearances were designed to convince lenders of his credit. But
wartime was not the time for reforms: he used all the established
tricks of the trade to bring in the funds. There is probably a lot of
truth in his claims that he put his profits at the service of the
monarchy in its hour of need. All the same, his lifestyle and wealth
made him an obvious target, if the crown should need one, to set
an example to others (**56**).

It is ironic that Colbert, whose family was later to become the
rival of the Le Telliers and who was himself to bring about the fall
and persecution of Fouquet, should have begun as a client of Le
Tellier and the man who recommended Fouquet to him! That says
as much about the man as it does about seventeenth-century
politics. Colbert too was the product of that ambitious sixteenth-
century bourgeoisie* that opted for royal service and had aristocratic ambitions. Again, family was important, as it has rightly been
said by J.L. Bourgeon that it was the Colberts who made Colbert
(**52**, ch. 5). Here was another clan that rallied its members to push

to the fore the most successful, so that he would be well placed to advance their own fortunes. The Colbert family came from Reims where they were wholesale cloth merchants on an international scale, with investments in office as well, and a highly profitable sideline in merchant-banking. By the 1620s the family had outgrown Reims and moved in 1630 to Paris, where in 1632 Nicolas Colbert bought for 350,000 *livres** the office of payer of *rentes**, which established him as a royal banker. As with Fouquet, since honesty was so relative, it would be unfair to look too closely at his practices, and in any case he was careful not to leave too much evidence.

His son, Jean-Baptiste Colbert (1619–83), the future minister, had a mediocre education but benefited from the training he acquired in several financial posts. In 1640 he was a commissioner for the army and then, in the mid-1640s, thanks to the influence of his cousin, de Saint-Pouange, who worked for Le Tellier, he became an aide to the war minister. During the *Frondes** he was the trusted go-between for Le Tellier and Mazarin, and in 1651 Mazarin asked Le Tellier to 'give' him Colbert. He soon won Mazarin's confidence and was entrusted with the care and development of the Cardinal's personal fortune. Astute investment, corruption and shady deals were his stock in trade (Mazarin expected nothing less), and he succeeded so well that by 1661 Mazarin had the largest private fortune of the *ancien régime**. Colbert knew how to be the perfect servant of his master – this was as true of his service to Mazarin as to Louis XIV – and the Cardinal passed him on to Louis at the time of his death. Louis employed him to explain and secretly supervise the royal finances in the summer of 1661, which gave Colbert the opportunity to reach high office at the expense of Fouquet.

Colbert worked prodigiously hard, from morning till night, writing almost all important dispatches himself and closely controlling all his subordinates. Although he submitted reports and orders for expenditure to the King in his working sessions with him, because Louis trusted him entirely, Colbert really was the complete master of the finances from the fall of Fouquet. Yet, he only acquired the title of controller-general in 1665, when he also became superintendant of buildings and of commerce, all these charges being a reflection of his existing power. Four years later he was appointed secretary of state for the marine and the royal household. His power reflected his place in the King's confidence as well as his capacity for hard work. Even so, when he became too attached to his own point of view, and forgot himself in council, he provoked the now famous letter of rebuke from the King:

> I was master enough of myself the day before yesterday to conceal from you the sorrow I felt in hearing a man whom I had overwhelmed with benefits... speak to me in the way you did. I have been very friendly towards you.... I still have such a feeling, and I believe that I am giving you real proof of it by telling you that I restrained myself for a single moment for your sake.... I did not wish to tell you what I am writing to you, in order not to give you a further opportunity to displease me.... It is the memory of the services that you have rendered me, and my friendship, which have caused me to do so. Profit thereby and do not risk vexing me again, because after I have heard your arguments and those of your colleagues, and have given my opinion on all of your claims, I never wish to hear more about it .... I am telling you my thoughts so that you may work on an assured basis and so that you will not make any false steps (**47**, ch. 12, p. 203).

Louis here speaks as a master who is determined to be obeyed. However : ached Colbert was to his reform projects and to his balancing of receipts and expenditure, he had to give way. During the Dutch War of 1672–78, the controller-general was reduced to the usual expedients of his predecessors to find money. After the war, when the cost of building operations kept expenditure ahead of receipts, his disposition soured notably; the work seemed to verwhelm him and his morose air became more pronounced. There were therefore rumours of an imminent disgrace, shortly before his death in 1683 (**54, 53**).

If it is true that the Colbert family made Colbert, it is equally true that the minister was responsible for raising his family to the loftiest heights. He placed members of it in offices that he could thereby control. His brother, Colbert de Croissy (1625–96), became an intendant*, was entrusted with several delicate diplomatic tasks and succeeded Pomponne as secretary of state in 1679. His uncle, Henri de Pussort, tried to direct the *chambre de justice** in the 1660s and was important in the elaboration of the legal codes (**80**). One son was given a distinguished ecclesiastical career; another, the Marquis de Seignelay (1651–90), was groomed for succession as secretary of state for the marine and became a minister in 1689 (**80**). Three sons died in royal service in the wars. Colbert's daughters were married into the highest families of the peerage, with strong encouragement from the King, whose policy seemed to be to knit together the loyal families of the high robe and the high aristocracy, to form a political clan in his service. One daughter married the Duc de Beauvillier, later a minister, and another the Duc de Chevreuse, one of the King's trusted informal advisers. Several more distant relatives became intendants, and the numerous clients of Colbert were used to fill other offices. The historian of his clan considers that 'the size of the kingdom and the relative weakness of the administrative structures, necessitated this recourse to vast clienteles of relations, allies and protégés' (**52**, ch. 5, p. 90).

The third great family of robe or administrative nobility was the Phélypeaux. It was composed of two ministerial branches, the La Vrillière and the Pontchartrain (**78**). From the time of Henri IV until the end of the old regime there was always one member in office. Like the other dynasties, they began their rise in the sixteenth century, and came from the heartland of France, the region of Tours and Blois. The family began to acquire legal and financial offices, and Raymond II Phélypeaux, seigneur* of La Vrillière, became a treasurer-general and then secretary of state in 1621. During Louis' reign Phélypeaux de Châteauneuf, Marquis de La Vrillière (1638–1700) was a secretary of state (**80**). The Pontchartrains were related to the Maupeous, and thus to Fouquet, whose mother was a Maupeou. They naturally profited from these financial connections, and Pontchartrain, a president of one of the chambers in the parlement*, did his best to protect 'the partisans*', and particularly, those who had made their way in financial affairs in the last fifteen or twenty years, in whose favour he declared himself in all meetings, as his daughter-in-law's grand-father was one of them' (**1**, VII, pp. 213–18). According to a recent historian, these temporarily embarrassing connections neverthe-less ensured protection at court, where many other families had been involved with Fouquet's system. The Le Tellier family aided the return to favour of the Pontchartrains in 1677. Thus the Pontchartrains proved the worth of a network of financiers, courtiers and *parlementaires*; the subsequent career of Louis de Pontchartrain as controller-general (1689–99) and chancellor (1699–1714) reflected these very connections (**79**).

Clearly, these ministers by no means deserve the description of *bourgeois gentilhommes* which so many historians have accepted. It must also be recognised that the nobility itself was no longer the closed, exclusive group it liked to portray itself as, and that probably a good half of the late seventeenth-century nobility was of recent origin. The ministers' own recent origins therefore now look more typical of a large section of the legitimate nobility. To be sure, the ministers were not nobles of ancient stock, nor were they nobles of the sword*; rather, they were distinguished nobles of the robe* who owed their rise to loyalty and service to the crown. They were neither dukes and peers, but nor were they bourgeois*: they were members of a new group that the monarchy chose to employ (**44**, ch. 5). They were rewarded with marriages into the older and higher court nobility, and these marriages reflected not their lineage but their power and wealth. By the end of Louis' reign they were fully assimilated to the higher nobility. Thus a new group of high robe nobility was advanced by Louis XIV. Composed more or less of three great clans, from which he recruited his high officers of state, it was a group Louis considered to be far more dependable than members of his own extended family, who might harbour royal ambitions.

> To be perfectly honest with you, it was not in my interest to choose persons of greater eminence. It was above all necessary to establish my own reputation and make the public realise, by the very rank of those whom I selected, that it was not my intention to share my authority with them. (**7**, p. 35)

All the same, it was thought natural that these families should acquire the wealth and influence that were the fruits of office. While their loyalty to the monarch was unquestionable, their rivalry with one another was a major fact of political life. In order to avoid falling into the hands of a single faction, Louis had to play off two factions against each other. He speaks of this in his *Mémoires* in the context of seeking trustworthy advice. The Colbert and the Le Tellier families rivalled each other for high offices and took care to appoint members of their own extended family or their clients to posts within their purvey. Thus the navy was Colbertian and the army controlled by clients of Louvois, while the various intendants* tended to owe loyalty to either one or the other minister. For example, the intendant Nicolas-Joseph Foucault, a client of Colbert, found his career nearly broken and certainly his rise stopped after the death of his patron in 1683 and the subsequent enmity of Louvois.

At a higher level still, the conflicts between ministers often took the form of struggles to expand influence over decisions or appointments at the expense of the rival minister. Thus, Colbert succeeded in taking over the chancellor's role in appointing masters of requests* to jobs in the 1660s. Charles Frostin has shown that conflicts between ministers over their respective but often overlapping spheres of administration were very frequent later in the reign (**79**). The fact is, the functions and jurisdiction of offices were not clearly defined in this period (in spite of what we are so often told about the rise of an administrative monarchy), and it was still the man who made the office and not the office which made the man.

What must never be forgotten, and what comes out clearly in any examination of the rise to power of families, is that politics took place in the arena of the court. The court had originally been the royal household, which meant that it was at once the king's home and also the seat of his government. This dual function remained its characteristic, but the court by its size and permanence outstripped its function as home and greatly developed its function as instrument of government (**69, 70**). The idea that the Renaissance or modern state was essentially bureaucratic and administrative has been sharply challenged by historians who point out that the court was the nerve centre of the whole system. It was the centre of patronage without which government could not function, for patronage oiled the wheels of bureaucracy – indeed, it permeated the whole system. The administration thus had to function in the context of the court, whose values were very different (**20, 32**).

Little can be understood about the politics and conflicts of the era without taking the court into account. For the nobility, access to the King was to be had through court or household offices, and access to the King made it easy for courtiers to request favours for themselves or their clients. This enabled the King to exploit as fully as possible his ultimate control over the acquisition of offices and to hold families enmeshed in a web of royal patronage. It was a system that relied more on mutual benefits than on a clear triumph of the King over the nobility, because the King needed his nobles not only as an audience for his theatre of power but also as clients who could use their own influence over men to help him govern. Thus the high nobles, still influential in the provinces, requested favours which enhanced their prestige and therefore encouraged the provincial officials to respect and obey them and the King. Conversely, the King could not afford to be arbitrary in his treatment of members of leading families by refusing graces and favours, because he would thereby attack their honour, in refusing what was thought to be their due. Nor did he have an entirely free choice of candidates for high offices, being restricted to choosing between those families which were already powerful. A delicate balance was needed, a balance that could only be kept with the hand of a skilled master. If Louis appeared at times to be severe and unpredictable, this was in order to emphasise his position as supreme arbiter.

This exploitation of patronage and favour was standard early-modern practice (**99**), but Louis developed his courtly role still further. No one ever had a greater talent than Louis for making subtle distinctions of rank and favour in order to create a veritable political currency. In effect, and no doubt only half consciously, he tied honour more closely to royal favour, thus creating a kind of reflected glory. Not only were offices to be coveted, but also the royal greeting, the short conversation, the pleasant reference to a valorous deed, or a mere recognition [**doc. 4**]. The finest shades of rank were marked by Louis, who had a prodigious memory for faces and for the history of the many noble lineages. But favours were to be paid for by constant attendance, and everyone knows Louis' famous reply to a courtier soliciting a favour for an absentee: 'He is a man I never see.' The high nobility was in this way not so much depoliticised or rendered powerless, as kept under strict surveillance. A new bargain was emerging between ruler and aristocracy. During the course of Louis' long reign it became clear to everyone that there were richer rewards to be had from coopera-tion than from resistance. In particular, as Dessert has so clearly shown, the court served as the financial centre of the realm, with the rich pickings from royal war loans finding their way into the pockets of the aristocracy (**140**). Historians of this period are beginning to ask again whether it was Louis who dominated the court or the court which was the focal point of a whole aristocratic system of government. In fact, both are true. What has never been doubted is the mastery of Louis XIV in the role of courtier-king.

For this reason the several mistresses kept by Louis never had any decisive political weight, not even Madame de Maintenon (1635–1719) in the second half of his reign (**55**). On the other hand, Louis elevated the families of his mistresses, both their children and relatives, to high rank at court by conferring all sorts of favours on them. They thus took part in the politics of the court in ways that might have political repercussions. Since they had frequent access to the King it was possible for them to support certain families, who might more easily obtain ambassadorships, governorships or household offices. Louis created a dukedom for the house of Louise de La Vallière, his first mistress, but this was a mistake he did not repeat. His children by Madame de Montespan were married into the house of Bourbon; a niece of Madame de Maintenon was a married to a Noailles. These are exceptions, however, for in general Louis was at pains to preserve the social hierarchy, especially within the nobility. The only mistress to have real, if obscure, influence was Madame de Maintenon, but here again her sway was in the realm of appointments and putting favoured candidates before the King, rather than in decision-making [**docs 13, 14**]. Her religious devotion made her a channel for Jesuit influence in the later period, while earlier she had supported the Colberts against the Le Telliers. But neither minister nor mistress was ever allowed to usurp the role of king in affairs of state. It is evident that Louis was determined to be his own first minister, and that he never wavered in this desire.

3 The Years of Reform

In 1661, France was still exhausted after the effort needed to win the war against Spain. The monarchy was hugely in debt to the financiers and had anticipated the revenue for 1662 and 1663. The very bad harvest of 1661 created a famine in 1661–62 which worsened the plight of the peasantry, still greatly overburdened by royal taxation [**doc. 1**]. It has been estimated that 1.6 million people died during the dearth, which was probably the worst of the century. There was need for a period of peace in which to pay due attention to domestic affairs. Trade had to be given a chance to recover from the effects of war, the excessive weight of taxation needed to be reduced and the truly chaotic and corrupt financial practices needed to be curtailed. In the eyes of the King, the years of war had enabled the social groups and corporations to take advantage of weakened royal authority, to increase their power and independence. Such a situation not only offended Louis' classical sense of order and hierarchy, but it also reflected a lack of sufficient respect for the monarchy. Louis' first priority, therefore, as befitted a ruler who aimed to be a great and glorious monarch, was to restore order in the kingdom (**7**).

Finance

The most pressing reforms which were needed were financial. According to Colbert's estimate, the debts of the crown amounted to 451 million *livres** in 1661. The revenue from the tax farms was supposed to bring in 36,858,000 *livres*, but nearly 26 million of this was consumed by the costs of collection, which were extremely high, and payments to creditors with *rentes** and pensions. Dent and his successors have shown that the financial system in force during the wars was incapable of preventing corruption and malad-ministration (**134, 138–9**). The usual remedy was to hold a *chambre de justice**, a special court, to fine and punish the financiers who had made excessive profits, and thereby introduce some order while reducing the royal debt (**140**, chs 11 and 12). Good reasons existed, therefore, for a judicial inquiry. However, appearances can be deceptive, and this was never more true than in the world of government finance. What was presented as a simple prosecution and reform of abuses had hidden motives. Colbert was the guiding spirit behind it all, and his own aims were far from pure.

In 1661, with the death of Mazarin, Colbert lost his patron even though he gained a more important one in the King. But his position must have appeared precarious. He was the man most closely involved in amassing Mazarin's prodigious fortune (100 million *livres**) during the very years of penury for the state. Clearly, if questions were to be asked, he, with his own recent wealth, would be in an awkward position. It must have seemed that unless the blame for the state's finances could be laid at the door of Fouquet, who knew everything, Colbert and Mazarin would be held responsible – and Mazarin could no longer protect Colbert. Since 1658 at least Colbert had become Fouquet's deadly rival, and he engaged in a sequence of none-too-honest denunciations of Fouquet, first to Mazarin and then to Louis, whose confidence he quickly gained. There were additional reasons which must have made Louis decide to act swiftly. Fouquet was clearly marked out by character and experience for high office, but his display and ambition made Louis afraid of him (in spite of his proven loyalty), and he seemed not to take seriously Louis' desire to have no first minister. In addition, Fouquet had loaned the crown at least 6, possibly 12, million *livres*, on his personal credit. If he could be made the scapegoat for a whole system this would preserve Mazarin's reputation, protect numerous courtiers (including Colbert himself), eliminate a potentially dangerous minister, and cancel a significant portion of the royal debt.

Nothing less than the death penalty would suit the King and his new minister. Louis' decision to move against Fouquet was taken in April or May 1661, and the summer was spent preparing the ground. The approval of the Queen-Mother, Anne of Austria, was sought, while Fouquet was encouraged to borrow money for the crown on his own credit and to divest himself of an office in the Paris parlement* that would have protected him during a trial. The famous fête which Fouquet gave in honour of the King at his splendid château of Vaux-le-Vicomte in August, and which is often said to have offended Louis by its ostentation, was merely a further justification for the arrest. This took place on 5 September 1661, in a scene which provided the world with confirmation of the King's capacity for discretion, not to say duplicity (**56**).

33

Analysis

The *chambre de justice**, which was set up with a very wide purview to impose fines on financiers, lasted from 1661 until 1665 and was scarcely more honest. Nearly 500 people were fined a total of 156,360,000 *livres**, of which two-thirds was paid by eighty-seven individuals (**138**, ch. 6). The clients and favourites of the King and Colbert got off very lightly – although some of these old scores were settled after Colbert's death – but the financial network of Fouquet was destroyed. As Dessert has shown, Colbert was in the process of eradicating a rival financial clientele in order to replace it over the next few years with one of his own (**141**). Never was the saying 'Plus ça change, plus c'est la même chose' more true than of these political manipulations. The other important aim was to conduct a partial and disguised bankruptcy, by cancelling the debts the monarchy could not afford to pay. This was successful, but it was clear from 1662 that too much persecution would ruin the future credit of the monarchy, since ultimately it needed the very people it was prosecuting. Meanwhile, the trial of Fouquet was not going well, in spite of the determined efforts of the prosecutors, some of whom had been hand-picked by Colbert and were directed by his uncle. All Paris was agog at the struggle in the courts, where Fouquet, even though forbidden access to documents, put up a brilliant defence (**12**). Most of the magistrates were too honest to condemn a man to death on evidence that was either non-existent, inconclusive or clearly falsified. The verdict was not death but exile, and Louis, displeased, personally and arbitrarily condemned his former minister to perpetual imprisonment in the fortress of Pignerol, where he remained until his death in 1680 (**56**).

Colbert was by then well established in the confidence of his king and was genuinely motivated by ideas of reform. He has often been credited with having had in mind a 'system' – that is, a set of plans and a doctrine – and many historians have seen him as an innovator attempting a revolution from above. The reality was more prosaic. Few of Colbert's ideas were original, whether in the realm of administration, finance or commerce. In a theoretical sense, he therefore had no system, for he was a practical man who liked to base his decisions on the information he was constantly demanding of his subordinates. If he seemed protectionist, it was merely to protect his new manufactures; if he seemed 'mercantilist', this term is merely an economic historian's rationalisation of ideas and assumptions that were widely accepted in the seventeenth century (**52**, ch. 4; **54**) and in any case Colbert did not put the interests of commerce before those of agriculture; if he seemed to have instigated an administrative revolution, he was merely carrying on the ideas of previous superintendants, and this is as true in the realm of the arts as of the intendants*. Colbert was, however, very much more strict and systematic than his predecessors, and was entirely devoted to the *gloire**of the monarchy. In the words of the colloquy held to commemorate the tercentenary of his death:

> In the present state of research, historians accept the picture of a Colbert who was careful, hard-working, intelligent, well-informed and supple, who could see what he wanted very clearly, but who would modify his conceptions in accordance with the needs of the moment and the experience acquired from the facts.(**52**, ch.1, p. 26)

Tithes, indirect taxes, *rentes**, the General Farm*

In 1658, Fouquet had begun the reduction of the *taille**, from 50 million *livres** to 42, and Colbert reduced it by a further 3 million for 1662. This was not only because of the penury and famine pressing on the peasantry but also because loans had been guaranteed on the strength of the *taille* and they could not be paid on non-existent receipts. The manoeuvre was a further element in the partial bankruptcy, therefore. From 1658 to the mid-1660s the *taille* was reduced from 50 million *livres* annually to 32 million. With a view to the longer term, a lot of attention was paid to the exorbitant costs of collection, occasioned by the fraudulent practices of royal agents (**142**) and reluctance to pay on the part of the overburdened peasants. Colbert reduced the fees taken by the receiver of tithes from 25 per cent to 3.75 per cent of all tax paid, and used the intendants* to root out many malpractices. In 1670 he could claim with justified satisfaction that the *taille,* when at the wartime level of 52 million, had yielded only 16 million for the treasury, whereas it now produced 24 million from a levy of 32. Still part of the measures taken to reduce the royal debts were the arbitrary reductions in interest on royal loans guaranteed by various institutions such as the Paris municipality: *rentes sur l'Hôtel de Ville*. On the grounds that contracts had been made at exorbitantly high rates of interest during the wars, some *rentes* were cancelled and others rescheduled at a very low rate of interest. The results of all this activity were remarkable. In 1661 about 27 million *livres* had to be paid each year in interest on the debts, but by 1683, even after the Dutch War, this amount had been reduced to only 8 million. In the ten years from 1661 to 1671, net revenues had increased from 31,845,038 *livres* (according to Fouquet) to 75,433,497 *livres* (according to Colbert).

Several further measures were taken to create a sounder financial system. The periodic and much resented *recherches de noblesse* were intended to weed out false nobles claiming unjust tax exemptions – although they were later to become simply another way of making families pay for the confirmation of their titles. The intendants* were given wide powers to oversee the collection of the *taille** and impose their own assessments on the undertaxed. In spite of the pressure by the intendants (see below), it was never possible during the *ancien régime** to prevent the rich and powerful from enjoying greater exemptions than were lawful, because they were powerful enough to intimidate or ignore the local opposition. One sensible and partial solution to this was to move more towards indirect taxes paid by all. Colbert therefore increased the weight of the various indirect taxes compared with the direct ones. At the same time he reorganised the collection of many of them, already in the hands of numerous tax farms, into one ensemble, the General Farm*, with a single lease. He was thus able to impose better book-keeping, less fraud and consequently a higher price, while forcing a cut in costs. The first of the great tax farms in 1681 was sold for 56,670,000 *livres** annually, and this sum was subsequently increased (**137**).

Administrative order: parlements*, intendants*, provincial assemblies

Financial order went hand in hand with administrative order. It was not possible to prevent abuses in the fiscal system without having both the fullest information on the regions and a corps of officials able to exert pressure. The role of the intendants*, or commissioners on mission, as Colbert preferred to call them, lay precisely in this domain. Although the intendants had been temporarily abolished during the *Frondes**, they had reappeared under Mazarin with specific missions and instructions to be more sensitive to local officeholders by not usurping their functions (**86**). Colbert greatly added to their role and made them into the most important agents of the royal government. He heaped task after task upon them, demanding constantly that they redouble their efforts, while providing them with letters of commission with wide powers to report on corruption and pressurise local officials.

The intendants* were the eyes and ears of the central government. Colbert was systematic in his projects for reform, and he wanted them to be based on as full a knowledge of the differing local situations as possible. He instigated great *enquêtes* (inquiries) into the local economies, the types of manufacture, commerce, local judicial practices and the local power structures, with details of the men and families of influence [**doc. 12**]. In spite of the varying quality of the replies, never before had the monarchy had at its disposal such accurate information on which to base its policies. It was in keeping with Colbert's general approach that he and Louvois also began the systematic preservation of state archives.

The main practical duties of the intendants* were to oversee the collection of royal revenues, to ensure the liquidation of municipal debts and to root out corruption. They were given many other tasks, such as the organisation of local food supplies in times of dearth, but care was now taken not to interfere needlessly with the existing local authorities [**doc. 22**]. Intendants were severe in their repression of disorders occasioned by the collection of taxes, but also became to some extent the defenders of the peasants against the rapacity of the crown's fiscal agents. In this work they were largely successful – by old-regime standards. However, their determined attempts to regulate the problem of municipal debt, often cited as their most significant achievement, since it is said to have led to the extension of royal control over the towns, was largely a failure. Passive resistance from the municipalities was one reason for this, but more important was the extent and complexity of the problem. Finally, the government itself undermined its own reform: the need for further royal loans led to later controllers-general forcing the towns to lend to the government on their own credit, while the creation of new municipal offices during the later wars encouraged the councillors to use municipal funds to buy up the new offices that undermined their position. Nevertheless, during the years of Colbert the power and influence of the intendants were established to the extent that they became the principal arm of the state bureaucracy. Their importance as permanent representatives of the monarchy in the provinces was confirmed.

Royal policy towards the parlements* was a mixture of harshness and diplomatic compromise. There was no sentiment in this approach: 'I know my son', Louis wrote in his *Mémoires*, 'and can sincerely assure you that I feel neither aversion nor bitterness towards my judicial officers. On the contrary, if age is venerable in men, it appears all the more so to me in these ancient bodies' (**7**, p. 43). Even so, judicial wages were cut by a third, the council tried to avoid calling the parlements 'sovereign' courts, preferring 'higher courts', and some of the jurisdictional quarrels between courts, that so prejudiced business were put more firmly in the hands of the royal council [**doc. 27**]. In 1673, during the Dutch War, the courts were forbidden to remonstrate against royal letters patent without having registered them first, though it is significant that this the restriction did not apply to *ordonnances*, edicts and declarations (**32**; and **docs 25** and **26**). These measures were all designed to emphasise the supremacy of royal authority over the role and jurisdiction of the courts. On the other hand, as Hamscher has shown in a remarkable study of the Paris parlement, the edict of 1673 was drawn up after the royal policy of conciliation and compromise had been working for some years. Nothing fundamental was done to undermine the recruitment to the parlements (in other words, their oligarchical nature was respected) and they were extensively consulted on judicial reforms before these were promulgated (**64**). If the edict on remonstrances was not challenged until 1713, this was because the ministry became more sophisticated in avoiding clashes. Even the intendants* were warned to work with and not against the parlements [**doc. 22**]. The courts, in short, were tamed rather than subjugated.

The same may be said for the provincial estates which had put up such resistance to royal attempts to increase taxation from the 1630s. It is simply a distortion of the facts to claim, as so many historians have done, that the estates were stripped of their powers of resistance and reduced to a nominal role. It is true that where the central government could cow the estates into blind obedience, or where it was possible to cease calling the meetings without too much of an outcry, it was pleased to do so. Thus, the Estates of Provence were transformed into a rather more pliable Assembly of Communities, some smaller provincial assemblies were dropped altogether, and the estates of Normandy and Dauphiné were allowed to lapse. But it was impossible and unthinkable to suppress the powerful and useful estates of Brittany, Languedoc or Burgundy. Nor was there any strong desire to put an end to those in the newly conquered provinces such as Flanders, Artois or Franche-Comté; indeed, Roussillon, after its acquisition in 1659, was given its sovereign court (**83, 84, 96**). The principle of legitimacy, in a legitimate absolute monarchy, prevented even the King from attacking established rights. Troublesome though it was to manage the assemblies by choosing deputies where possible, by enticing them to obedience through the prestige and patronage of the governor, by bluffing them with fierce demands and shows of displeasure, the effort was worth it [**doc. 28**]. The reality was that the estates were too established in the legitimacy of the provincial mind and too useful as administrative bodies to part with (**83**). They therefore succeeded in protecting their provinces from the higher taxation in the *pays d'élection**, partly because their formal statements of submission cloaked implicit and sometimes quite overt bargains with the government about the confirmation of local rights and privileges*. Nevertheless, in comparison with the era of Richelieu and Mazarin, much progress had been made. The formal tone of submission that masked this reality helped to create that aura of monarchical grandeur that was so much a feature of Louis' reign.

Public order: revolts, the *Grands Jours*, the police, the legal codes

Where given an opening, Colbert and the King knew how to employ severity. The popular revolt in the Boulonnais is a fine example of this. Its origins were frankly political: the King could not easily attack established rights without just cause, but Louis admits in his *Mémoires* that he provoked the tiny province around Boulogne by imposing token taxes which symbolically contravened their legitimate privileges [**doc. 15**]. Naturally there was protest, which turned to revolt when the elite, no doubt secretly pleased at the turn of events, refused to intervene. Royal authority was being flouted at every turn; the fact that according to the norms of the time any other province would have reacted in the same way was precisely the reason for the whole affair. It is clear from the official correspondence that this was an opportunity not to be missed, for the Boulonnais could be an example to others [**doc. 16**]. The thirty-eight companies of soldiers subdued the revolt and the judicial repression began. The province was stripped of its privileges* and 1,000 men condemned. But the King knew how to temper justice with mercy. All those involved over seventy or under twenty-one were pardoned and only 400 sent to the galleys. This was the exact number required by the galley fleet.

There were to be many more outbursts of popular fury and

revolt before 1675: in fact, revolts are recorded in every year from 1660 to 1676 except 1667–68 and 1671 (**125**). Many were serious: for example, those in Gascony in 1664 about wine taxes, in Roussillon in 1666, in the Vivarais in 1670 – not to forget the revolt in Guyenne in 1674 which spread to Lower and Upper Brittany in the following year (**16**, ch. 8; **126**, **128**, **129**). The Breton revolt was in fact two, one being more urban and focused on privileges* and taxes, the other being more rural with significant anti-seigneurial* elements. The province had been heavily taxed from 1673 when the Estates had bought off new edicts, which were then reimposed in 1675, at a time when trade was hit by a prohibition on commerce with the Dutch. The peasants in any case lived under one of the harshest seigneurial regimes in France, and rents and dues were probably on the increase (a 'seigneurial reaction'). There was widespread revolt in the spring and summer of 1675, but the repression by the army commanded by the Duc de Chaulnes was so fearsome and well publicised that we may regard the subsequent calm as something of a triumph for the absolute monarchy.

Thus, although the army could never be an instrument of rule in a general sense, there is no doubt that the savage repressions by the royal troops were effective in discouraging open revolt after the 1670s. Certainly, sporadic outbreaks of popular violence continued to occur, but these were produced by the flaring of tempers under pressure (**132**). To ministers, it did not ever seem that victory was assured, and it was one of the duties of the intendant* to ensure the provisioning of towns and the maintenance of public order. The Camisard War in the Cévennes from 1702 was a different matter, being provoked by religious repression. But, in 1707, when taxes were at their highest, there were revolts against a rumoured tax on baptisms. The popular nature of these revolts may be studied in the fascinating elements of popular culture that characterise the assemblies [**doc. 18**].

A rough justice of a different order, equally necessary politically, was displayed in the much-needed special assizes of Poitou and the Auvergne (the *Grands Jours*). In September 1665 a special commission was sent down to Clermont to call to order the local nobility and clergy and judge their lawlessness. The peasantry had long been oppressed, and the area terrorised by the viciousness of many noble criminals who by their influence and intimidation were able to escape arrest and judgment in the local courts, where the officers were corrupt or powerless. An example was made of one of the most influential nobles, by rapidly judging and executing him. Terrified, many fled the royal justice, which, unable to catch them, then proceeded to dishonour them by executions in effigy. The resulting calm was a potent tribute to the restoration of royal authority. Naturally, as time passed and the costly expedient was not repeated, disorders gradually returned, although perhaps less extreme. It was bound to be so in a province 'as full of crime as this one', as the bishop Fléchier noted of the most important trial, where 'the prosecutor, the man who had investigated the case and the witnesses were all greater criminals than the defendant himself' (**9**). Such testimony serves to remind us of the magnitude of the problems facing the central administration.

Together with the imposition of order went the desire to see unified codes of law and legal practice drawn up and implemented. A wide range of provincial and customary law had survived the development of monarchical sovereignty, which made litigation and procedure an extremely complex affair. The codification undertaken in the sixteenth century had been at best partial. Colbert formed committees to study legal practice and draw up codes. In 1667 an ordinance for civil procedure was published; there followed in 1669 the ordinance on the rivers and forests, in 1670 the criminal code, in 1673 the commercial code, in 1672 and 1681 the maritime ordinances, and in 1685 the colonial code. Unfortunately, these met with traditionalist resistance from the courts and were never fully practised (**118**).

One reform that was both useful and effective was the creation of a new official jurisdiction for Paris. The still medieval city had outgrown its walls and a terrible confusion of public and private jurisdiction existed. Sanitary regulations were widely ignored, with the result that Paris was unhealthy, dangerous and filthy. The weight of the ministry brought about the revival of the authority of the Châtelet, the specifically Parisian court, and the overall power of the newly created (1667) lieutenant of police. Nicolas de La Reynie, the first such lieutenant, made the office into almost that of a secretary of state for the capital, so important and extensive were his duties. He was succeeded in 1697 by the equally competent Marquis d'Argenson (1697–1718). The spies employed by the lieutenants became a useful means of controlling opinion, frequent reports of which were sent to the King. It is proof of their efficacy that the police archives have been consulted as some of the best sources for most aspects of life in the capital, from everyday life to criminality.

Analysis

The economy

Colbert is most renowned for his attempts to develop commerce and the economy. He undertook this ambitious project in order to impart *gloire** to his master and strength to the state, for he was convinced that 'Commerce is the sinews of finance and finance is the sinews of war'. In effect, he wrote in 1664, 'Only the abundance of money in a state affects its grandeur and power' (**1**, ii, p. cclxix). Like his contemporaries, Colbert had an essentially static vision of the world economy, regarding both the quantity of money in circulation and the amount of trade by exchanges as capable of only slight increases. From this it logically followed that 'the quantity of money in the kingdom can only be increased if at the same time the same amount is taken from neighbouring states'. It was therefore necessary to attract money from other countries and try to keep it inside France [**doc. 19**].

This could be done in several ways. Luxury products from abroad, such as Venetian lace, should be discouraged by tariffs, and French artisans encouraged to produce the same goods, perhaps under the direction of foreign entrepreneurs. The quality of more basic goods such as textiles should be improved, in order to compete in foreign markets with Dutch and English cloths. Raw materials should be imported into France and finished goods discouraged. The colonies played an important part in this thinking, being sources of materials, such as sugar, tobacco and furs, and there was a marked expansion in French colonial activity during the reign (**117**, **118**, **121**).

Exports were the key to the problem of lack of specie, and thriving commerce would not only bring bullion to the country; it would also fill the King's treasury through taxes at the same time as it kept his subjects from idleness. It was equally important that the carrying trade which brought such profits to the Dutch should be taken over by French ships. Tariffs on goods brought by foreign ships were proclaimed in 1664 and 1667, aimed especially at the English and the Dutch. Colbert was prey to an intense sense of rivalry with the Dutch, whose commerce he was determined to ruin for the benefit of France. This required an expansion in the navy and in the merchant marine, which in turn required sailors to be trained and available. Finally, French men and women should be encouraged to engage in useful occupations; that is to say, agriculture, commerce, the army and the navy.

Colbert set about this huge programme of royal intervention

from the early 1660s. First of all, information on all aspects of the economy was necessary. The *Enquête* completed by the intendants* in 1664 is regarded as the first real survey of the state of French manufactures. Imperfect though it was in details, it did enable Colbert to work from a rough statistical basis to develop his plans rationally. Luxury products and the cloth industry particularly concerned him. Numerous specialised manufactures were set up with government aid and investment funds that were demanded from the royal entourage, financiers and merchants. The crown paid out about 20 million *livres** in twenty years. Foreign workers were paid a bounty and given privileges* in return for bringing their special skills to France, and capable masters were placed in control of the enterprises, which were at first subsidised. Like the masters and workers, the manufactures themselves benefited from monopolies and privileges. These exempted them from taxation and gave them a monopoly of production and a protected market in certain regions, sometimes in all of France.

It must not be imagined that these manufactures were anything like modern factories or even a stage in the industrialisation of France. They were set up on the same lines as existing enterprises, but were encouraged to use the latest methods. They were not factories, but artisanal collectivities, or simply a number of workshops distributed across a town. There were some notable successes. The Gobelins and Beauvais tapestry works fulfilled their role of producing high-quality goods to rival those imported, as did the Point de France Venetian-lace industry. The latter was established in several towns, such as Auxerre, Reims and Alençon. A fine mirror workshop was set up in Tourlaville in 1667. The Van Robais woollen manufacture of Abbeville employed more than 4,000 artisans and was as successful as the similar Villenouvelle enterprise in the Hérault.

At the same time, Colbert had several codes of regulations drawn up to raise the quality of French goods, the most famous being the code for the wool industry issued in 1669. He also created a company of inspectors to gather information, give advice and ensure quality control. Privileged* corporations were encouraged because they oversaw quality and made inspection easier. In Paris their number increased from 60 in 1672 to 129 in 1691. In the long run, these closed groupings were to slow down expansion and the development of new techniques, both of which developed more readily in a more liberal climate. But Colbert himself was not a doctrinaire *étatiste*: 'You can rest assured that, every time that I find a greater or an equal advantage in it, I do not hesitate to withdraw the privileges', he wrote. He was in favour of internal freedom of trade and consequently the removal of the tolls that made transport so expensive. Yet although he may reasonably be regarded as the fountainhead of the 'single duty project' espoused by numerous eighteenth-century reformers, the attainment of such an ideal was impossible during his own lifetime.

In order to encourage trading ventures in new areas, Colbert decided to set up overseas trading companies. The most famous was the East India Company, which lasted with considerable difficulty from 1664 until the 1780s; the West India Company was founded in the same year but was abolished in 1674; others had a more or less brief existence, such as the Levant Company and the Company of the North. They mostly did not survive very long, either because they failed as commercial ventures of their own accord, or because their privileges* and monopolies were withdrawn by the ministry. That is not to say that they were entirely unsuccessful. Their role in the eyes of Colbert was to set in motion an expansion of trade that should then develop essentially through the activities of private merchants. This seems to be what indeed happened, and so the modern argument that the companies were irrelevant, that royal impulse was of little importance compared to private initiative, may be overstated. Nevertheless, there was a great deal of unwarranted optimism on Colbert's part in believing that such companies, run for the most part by the Colbert 'lobby' of family and creatures who were not above corruption, could sensibly dent the well-organised trade of England and Holland. The reaction of France's commercial rivals soon forced Colbert to lower his prohibitive tariffs, with the result that competition fatally undermined his companies. The figures for foreign trade do show a slight increase during the reign, but government initiative almost certainly had little to do with this (**107, 117–22**).

In recent years, the economic plans of Colbert have been regarded with considerably more realism or scepticism than earlier. Indeed, his projects faced many problems, most of which derived from the prevailing social attitudes and structures. For instance, in spite of the encouragement merchants received to remain in trade by the ennoblement of some of them, and the parallel encouragement given to nobles to take past in wholesale commerce without the formal loss of status, both groups stuck to their traditional conceptions. Merchants preferred offices to commercial investment, and nobles remained convinced that any form of trade was unbecoming. In the early 1700s the merchant community even protested that nobles, being wealthier, should not be allowed to compete (**43**, ch. 9).

The guilds and municipalities resisted new practices, while artisans were not interested in changing their ways if the old products still sold. The best example of resistance is the town of Marseille, notoriously uncooperative, which undermined all Colbert's efforts to force it to alter its trading patterns in order to develop a thriving Levant trade in cloth from Languedoc. As Cole put it, the reforms were undermined by a 'massive wall of folk inertia' (**119**), and we may add that the baroque state simply lacked the power to overcome this. The final blow to most of the enterprises came with the cutting of subsidies, as Louis, never very interested in the economy, devoted his revenues to buildings and wars. For Colbert it was plainly an uphill struggle, in what, as historians of the Annales school have reminded us, was an extremely unfavourable overall context for economic development. It has even been suggested that most of the meagre progress made at the time of the reforms would have occurred without them (**117, 122**).

It was only in 1669 that Colbert became secretary of state for the marine, but his appointment was simply an acknowledgement of his considerable prior involvement. His dream, and one that was briefly to come true, was to create a navy that truly reflected the strength and the *gloire** of his king. In this he was following Richelieu, whose efforts had foundered for lack of money, and Fouquet, who had begun the task anew. The navy in 1661 consisted of rotting hulks and only eighteen serviceable ships of the line. From 1661 to 1671, 111 ships were built at Brest at the same time as the arsenal there was greatly developed; moreover, an entire new port was constructed at Rochefort from 1663. By 1683 the French navy was a substantial force, consisting of 117 ships and 30 galleys. Such an achievement implied the development of French supplies of sailcloth, munitions, tar – all that ships required, and especially timber for shipbuilding and trees suitable for masts. A whole policy of regulation and maintenance of forests was instituted (the Ordinance of 1669), though its success, for reasons that have already been suggested, was limited (**179, 181**).

The attempt to provide a supply of sailors for the fleet has been the subject of one of the finest and briefest detailed studies of resistance to the central government in this period (**178**). Colbert set up a system of three naval classes in which all sailors would be registered and from which, in turn, they would be called upon to man the fleet. The system was obviously much fairer than the press-gang and should have worked well. Unfortunately, it was undermined from all sides. The state itself undermined it by calling up the best sailors from all three classes during the Dutch War, and every conceivable kind of local, judicial and bureaucratic resistance arose. Even so, the policy of maritime classes was a great improvement on what had gone before and led to the greater availability of capable seamen. The fleet itself was able to prove its value in war by winning control of the Mediterranean in 1676 from the Spanish and Dutch, and by the victory off Beachy Head in 1690 against the combined English and Dutch forces. The tragedy was that Louis was never really interested in the navy and preferred to concentrate his foreign policy on land warfare, giving up the option of an overseas empire and naval strength in order to divert funds to the army. The naval budget was reduced during the 1680s and drastically cut after 1692 (**182**).

Art and architecture: the imagery of *gloire**

The reforms in administration and finance during Louis' reign have left, for those who do not look closely enough, the impression of a transformation of the state. This view has gained the credence it possesses not only because of a readiness to mistake administrative regulations for political reality, but also because of the enduring power of the image of the monarchy that was projected by patronage of the arts. The first decades of the personal rule are especially notable for the harnessing of the arts to the monarchy. Inspired by Richelieu – who had created the Academy, built the Palais Royal and the Château of Richelieu, with its gardens and attendant town – and by Mazarin, the great art collector, as well as by Fouquet, the creator of Vaux-le-Vicomte, Louis gave full rein to his passion for architecture in particular. But all the arts were put in the service of the King. Monarchy, art and propaganda had long been associated in Europe, and the Renaissance had led to a revival of classical imagery. Much of it is now fairly incomprehensible to an observer not steeped in the texts of the ancients and familiar with the notions of emblems and heraldic devices. Hardly anyone except scholars now reads Ovid's *Metamorphoses* and Cesare Ripa's *Iconologia* (1598), but they were tremendously influential in the seventeenth century, running through many illustrated editions. Classical mythology and fable were the basis of artistic culture (**196**). To understand what Louis achieved in the realm of the arts we must try to understand the contemporary values.

Two notions are particularly important. The first is the wide belief in the idea that the pagan gods had once been outstanding human beings, such as kings, whose veneration had led to their transformation into the gods of mythology. The *Annals* of Ennius conveyed this theory to the Renaissance, and led cultivated people to believe that such transformations were still possible – if the Roman emperors had believed it, why not the age of Louis XIV? A second element is the Neoplatonist convention that divine truth had to be veiled by a coded pictorial language, a kind of hiero-glyphics or iconology, such as that discussed in the handbook of Cesare Ripa, which is all about mythology. Thus the art and propa-ganda of Louis XIV must be set in the context of the Renaissance traditions developed by court society over at least a century (**202, 204**). This fact alone should be enough to convince us that, although Louis could show a preference for specific styles, the arts retained a certain autonomy during his reign. In other words, he made full use of existing traditions without himself revolutionising art any more than he did the state.

Amongst the cultured elite then, there was the widespread belief that images or emblems conveyed a message better than words. It was of course necessary for the King to have an emblem and a motto. The emblem that Louis made his own was therefore the sun, with a new motto, *Nec pluribus impar*: 'not unequal to many' [**doc. 6**]. No doubt Louis was influenced in his conduct by the attribution to him of the sun theme, and by its ambitious motto. As an image it was certainly effective. One contemporary wrote:

> Since the king has taken this star for his symbol, has so to speak appropriated it, those who are somewhat enlightened take the sun for him, and have present in their minds at the same time both one and the other. (**196**, p. 34)

Being the leading patron of the arts, Louis had ceaseless opportu-nity to exploit symbolism in the service of the monarchy. In art as in conduct, he constantly projected the image of a powerful king and a strong monarchy, a monarchy that was bound to defeat all opposition and rise to Olympian heights. These ideas were expressed in all the genres.

The *carrousel* and the official royal entry into Paris in 1660 and 1662 are justly famous as examples of the political use of festivity. The processions were the image of the social hierarchy, and the temporarily erected triumphal arches with their mythological decorations, the symbolism of grandeur, all combined to create a magnificent impression of the monarchy. The *carrousels* staged in Paris and, for the first time, at Versailles in 1664, were enormous pageants directed at the court, ambassadors and France. These displays were of a closed symbolic universe which celebrated and confirmed order and hierarchy. The visual display was always considered the most important form of expression, but it had the drawback of being ephemeral. For this reason, the message conveyed by a display, a ballet, an opera or a play was rendered durable by the other arts. Painting and poetry, for example, preserved the memory of the event and underlined its significance. This continuity in a different form resolved the dialectic between the ephemeral and the durable: writing (especially poetry), engraving, medals, painting, tapestry, sculpture, architecture, could be permanent records of the grandeur of the King (**196, 199, 201, 203, 210**).

In this world in which musical and visual forms were thought to be more important than the written, prose as a form was too humble to speak the glory of the King satisfactorily. Architecture and sculpture were the principal forms for impressing the royal grandeur upon the world. Louis did constantly express his own views, but it was Colbert, as superintendant of buildings, who was responsible for commissioning and overseeing the vast programmes [**doc. 5**]. The minister was therefore closely involved in the royal policy. Indeed, it could be argued that the relative collapse and confusion of artistic policy from the 1690s points to Colbert's decisive role as the real instigator of the monumental glorification of the King in the early decades (Schnapper in **209**). He expressed the guiding principle very clearly in a letter to Louis in 1665:

> Your Majesty knows that apart from brilliant military exploits, nothing testifies better to the grandeur and spirit of princes than buildings; and all posterity takes the measure of princes by the proud mansions that they have constructed during their lifetime. (**1**, v, p. 269)

Colbert, of course, wished to see Paris beautified by royal building projects, but Louis preferred the even more grandiose and expensive task of creating Versailles. The King's passion for architecture was such that every day for fifty years he spoke with his architects or gardeners. They were men of extraordinary talent: the team of Louis Le Vau (1612-70) and André Le Nôtre (1613–1700), who had created Vaux-le-Vicomte, were taken into the service of the King to create Versailles and several other châteaux with their gardens; Jules Hardouin-Mansart (1646-1708), who designed so much of Versailles, also built the châteaux of Marly, Saint-Cloud and Sceaux, as well as the dome of the Invalides and several town halls and squares. During the reign there was ceaseless building and reconstruction of the royal residences as well as work in Paris and the provinces. Much of this classical architecture has survived to this day; in the context of the disorder and poverty of the seventeenth-century towns, its effect was tremendous.

Nevertheless, most of the major achievements date from the early decades. The transformation of Versailles from the small hunting lodge of Louis XIII into the vast château and park we know today, took from 1661 to 1689 and occupied on average 25,000 workers a day. In the 1660s the Louvre, which was still the principal royal residence, was improved, by the addition of its colonnade, that masterpiece of classical architecture by Le Vau, and by the Gallery of Apollo; the Invalides was built from 1671 to 1675. The château of Marly, a smaller, more intimate residence consisting of a royal pavilion flanked by twelve smaller separate ones in a magnificent park, was constructed between 1679 and 1686; the Grand Trianon was built next door to the château of Versailles from 1687 to 1689. The expenditure on architecture was enormous, totalling about 200 million *livres*** during the reign. The Dutch War slowed the pace of building in the 1670s, but the Nine Years War and the War of the Spanish Succession created severe financial problems that put an end to major projects (**211**).

The buildings had to be in the appropriate setting, and thus *places royales* (royal squares) and especially gardens were important. Gardens revealed man's remodelling of disordered nature into a harmonious universe. For this, perspective was all-important (**215**). The garden would seem to join the sky at the end; tricks of perspective would blur the distinction between reality and illusion. These techniques added to the theatrical impression of being part of another, Olympian, world. Gilded statues were everywhere, portraying well-chosen scenes from mythology. Mirrors, too, were a feature, placed everywhere inside rooms, and could even be outside as in the Grotto of Thetis. Mirrors not only reflect but also have a magical quality about them. The basins and lakes in the gardens of the châteaux can be seen as mirrors, reflecting the statues and the sky, creating the impression that the world of the garden joined and reflected the heavens. Inside and outside, mirrors made the courtiers into actors in a world peopled by the gods, dominated by Apollo. The Hall of Mirrors at Versailles is just one example among many of the use of mirrors for interiors. There is, too, an element of theatre and mirror in the squares that were constructed in the towns. These *places royales* would normally have as their centrepiece a statue of the King, surrounded by uniform classical architecture. Famous surviving squares are the place des Victoires in Paris, the place des Etats in Dijon and the place Bellecour in Lyon. The square had the effect of turning the people in it into actors on a grand stage, of making life a theatre, in the presence of the King (**211**).

Gardens and theatre are closely linked in courtly culture, the gardens having theatrical elements in their composition and often serving as the actual place of performance for plays, ballets and diversions. The cleverly created perspectives that were a feature of these gardens could become a backdrop for theatrical events like the Pleasures of the Enchanted Island, a grand fête in 1664. The Grotto of Thetis at Versailles was used as a theatre set, in 1674, for Molière's *Malade imaginaire*. In 1667 the *Ballet de la jeunesse* used the Fountain of Latona and the château of Versailles itself as a backdrop, while the *cour de marbre* was used to stage operas. A consequence of this was that the distance between the audience and the players was not psychologically as great as it is today; indeed, the courtiers saw aspects of their world represented either literally (as in Molière) or allegorically (as in Racine) (**200**). This point is reinforced by the fact that court society was a society that played itself theatrically, constantly watching itself, constantly performing stylised activities. It is hardly necessary to dwell upon the theatricality of the royal *lever* and *coucher* (when courtiers with privileged access to the King waited upon him in a highly regulated ceremony when he arose or prepared to retire to bed), while the royal meals served and eaten in public to the accompaniment of music were closely related to ballet.

The perfect combination of theatre, poetry, dance and music was to be found first in ballet and then, from the 1670s, in opera. Until 1670 Louis danced in several ballets before the court (**197**). These masked ballets both represented the harmony and order of the universe, by which everything was held in perfect relation, and portrayed the royal family and the court in submission to the Sun

King. In a series of operatic masterpieces, Lulli (1634–87) and Quinault (1635–88) sang the praises of the King in tales from mythology, chiefly by Ovid, which were given an overt contemporary significance. Isherwood emphasises the political role of such entertainments:

> The operas of Lulli and Quinault began with prologues that were transparent allegorical tales acted out by gods, nymphs, and demons, in which the official history of Louis' reign unfolded. They not only presented encomiums to the monarch, they also alluded to Louis' latest military exploits. They literally interpreted his foreign policy and the wars to audiences, always stressing the evil designs of his enemies and the heroism, courage, magnanimity, and justice of the king of France. (**209**, p. 142; and **208**)

Official painting was dominated by the figure of Charles Le Brun, First Painter to the King (1619–90). His first masterpiece for Louis – an allegory of royal virtue and self-control – depicted Alexander the Great visiting the wife and daughters of the captured King Darius. It struck exactly the right note, for Louis was delighted by the theme, and Versailles rapidly became Le Brun's canvas. In paintings too numerous to mention – though we could never omit the Hall of Mirrors and the Salons of War and Peace – he portrayed the glories and virtues of the King in allegories taken from mythology or antiquity. As in the sculpture of the château and park, Alexander, Apollo, Jupiter, Mars, Hercules and their exploits are everywhere. If Versailles was a mirror of antiquity it was also a temple to Louis XIV. Other paintings were on display, too, by Raphael, Correggio, Titian, Veronese, Poussin, to name but a few. We should perhaps make a distinction between what was on display as movable art and the permanent décor : Louis XIV was a collector, so many of the paintings were simply some of the finest Renaissance art, acquired and exhibited by the monarch as part of the traditional policy of royal display (**209**, **214**).

The significance of Versailles should now be apparent. In style and conception it was a part of a vast project to exploit the arts in the service of the King. The buildings and gardens created a classical world, illustrated and reinforced by painting and sculpture, in which a certain image of royalty was projected. Great emphasis was put upon the virtue and the power of the King, ruling over an ordered universe. The arts contributed to the grandeur of the King, and transmitted the memory of his exploits to future generations. In fact, without this memory there could be no true grandeur (**212, 213**). This was not a new conception; what is new about the artistic patronage of Louis XIV is its scale, for Versailles is distinguished by its gigantic proportions. The display of power could therefore take place in theatrical surroundings that were designed to overawe the spectator. Foreign ambassadors, in particular, were extremely impressed.

This courtly grandeur should be seen as a vital aspect of Louis' baroque state, as display, representation and pageant created an aura of power. The court of Versailles was at the centre of the governing system, the meeting point for King, courtiers, ministers, ambassadors and deputations from the provinces. But the grandiose château lends itself to interpretation on many levels. It also reflects a move by King and court from Paris, that turbulent capital, where the Louvre stirred unpleasant memories for Louis as well as presenting aesthetic problems of remodelling and joining-up to the Tuileries, because of its awkward angled ground-plan. In contrast, Versailles was a palace of unparalleled grandeur befitting a king obsessed with his *gloire**; the fact of its construction in a marshy valley only emphasised his power. Here was an opportunity to create a court in his own style and image, one that can be described as classical-baroque. The exterior is largely classical, but inside it is essentially baroque, with scenes from Ovid's *Metamorphoses* everywhere [**doc. 7**]. What Colbert succeeded in doing for Louis XIV was orchestrating a style that posterity would identify with the 'Age of Louis XIV' or the 'Age of Grandeur'. To be sure, it was one deeply rooted in previous traditions, but it was also the culmination of these traditions in a powerful classical-baroque form. The *vrai* and the *beau* were successfully combined in all the arts. It was a style for *honnêtes hommes*, a style that was based on the ideology adopted by the monarchy: harmony and order.

Intrinsic to the development of this style was artistic control and patronage, in which the establishment of royal academies played an important part. In 1635 Richelieu had created the French Academy with the aim of linking culture more closely to the monarchy, and an Academy of Painting and Sculpture had been set up in 1648, but Colbert reorganised it in 1663–64: Le Brun (1619–90) controlled most of the patronage in the arts, and presided over a team of professors who gave lectures. The so-called 'Petite Académie' of 1661, drawn from the Academy to devise royal inscriptions, became the Academy of Inscriptions and Belles-Lettres in 1663. The year 1666 witnessed the creation of the

Academy of Sciences; 1669, the Royal Academy of Music, under Lulli; and 1671, that of the Royal Academy of Architecture. The purpose of these institutions was to distinguish the higher arts from the mechanical ones by elaborating doctrine and teaching theory in an intellectual way. They thus became promoters of research, arbiters of taste and centres of patronage – but also focal points for provincial loyalties.

Belles-lettres flourished in these years to an almost unsurpassed degree. In literary terms, this was the age of Molière (1622–73), Racine (1639–99), Corneille (1606–84), La Fontaine (1621–95), La Bruyère (1645–96) and Perrault (1628–1703) – authors whose works have become classics which are still read or performed. Their contemporaries included writers and preachers such as Boileau (1636–1711), Fontenelle (1657–1756), Fénelon (1651–1721) and Bossuet (1627–1704) who were all greatly influential in their time. King and ministers protected and gave patronage to these men, much of whose production combined royal flattery with art of the highest order. Tragedies, comedies and satire tended to conform to the classical rules but rose far above mere eulogies of the King by providing profound insights into the human heart, by dealing with the universal in a morally uplifting way. For this reason the best literature deserves to be called classical. However, its influences and tendencies are far too complex and varied to be ascribed to the action of the King. His was, in this sphere, a patronage that allowed artistic genius to flourish and thus redound to his credit (**194**).

Royal policy was behind the vast mass of propagandist literature that flowed from the presses in Louis' reign (**202**). It was not propaganda in the modern sense, for it was designed to inform and praise. There were numerous accounts of battles, histories, panegyrics of the King, descriptions of the royal achievements in architecture, of the fêtes and entertainments. *Te deums* in cathedrals and churches celebrated royal victories in war, sermons preached obedience and choirs sang the royal praise. Strangely enough, hardly any of this was specifically directed outside France, as Klaits has shown in his study of printed propaganda (**184**). Tracts designed to present French policy in a favourable light to non-French audiences made a late appearance; not until Colbert de Torcy became foreign secretary during the War of the Spanish Succession did French propagandists attempt a conquest of opinion abroad. By that stage it had become necessary to counter the vast quantity of anti-French literature flowing from the periodical presses of England and Holland. We may conclude from this that Louis' prime interest was in controlling France and assuring his *gloire** at home. Only when foreign publications began to influence French opinion was it necessary to retaliate.

The artistic and political achievements of the King were diffused throughout France and Europe by means of medals, engravings and paintings. More than 130 medals were struck, and countless engravings were made of major works of architecture, sights, pageants, paintings and tapestries (**203, 201**). They were accompanied by texts writtten for the most part by that indefatigable propagandist Félibien. As he himself wrote, 'by means of these prints all nations will admire the sumptuous edifices that the king has constructed regardless of cost, as well as the rich ornaments that embellish them' (**209**, p. 122).

The essential point often missed in numerous otherwise admirable studies of art and literature is that the arts did not reflect the reality of royal power, but were a part of the government's attempt to create that very illusion. The use of art for the purpose of glorification and propaganda presupposes that there are people who need to be convinced. In the event, those people were the European statesmen and the French nation. However, the same techniques and artistic language could also be turned against the royal propaganda, by local elites wedded to their provincial traditions. They would delay the implementation of royal projects and attempt to evade the installation of the ubiquitous statues of the King (**195**). As it happened, Louis was to be more successful with historians than with his contemporaries.

The price of glory

There was a price to be paid for Louis' display and grandeur. The financial reforms and the recourse to extraordinary measures had enabled Colbert to pay for the Dutch War. What worried him most was the extravagance of royal policy in peacetime. In 1680 he wrote to the King the following oft-cited letter:

> I beg your Majesty to read these few lines with some reflection.... After eight to nine years of war and an expenditure of 110 to 120 million each year, Your Majesty had anticipated only 22 millions on the following years (revenue).... In 1680, spending exceeds receipts by 20 millions and Your Majesty will still owe....12 to 13 millions.... Your Majesty's revenue, because of the reductions he has made to his people, come to 65

or 66 million livres. I have them recorded as 70 millions, and, subtracting 6 or 7 millions in debts whose payment can be postponed, out of the revenues for 1681 only 22 or 23 million will remain for expenditure. This means that we must be prepared to draw on the revenue for 1682 from next March or April.... I well know, Sire, that the problem can be explained, but it is necessary to find solutions.... In my view, Sire, all that can be said on the matter can only lead to increasing the receipts and reducing expenditure. As for increasing the receipts, I can only say to Your Majesty that it is to be feared that I might go too far, and that the prodigious increase in the tax farms be too much of a burden on the populace....concerning expenditure, although it is not my business at all, I only beg Your Majesty, to allow me to say that in war as in peace, He has never consulted his finances before resolving on expenditure, which is so extraordinary that assuredly there are no other examples of it. (1, II, i, pp. ccliv–vi)

In the short term, Colbert was successful. Never before had a French monarch ruled over such an ordered state, nor had such riches at his disposal for public works and glorious enterprises. Yet the very fact that Colbert was willing to sacrifice his own long-term reform plans, such as they were, in order to sustain the King's quest for *gloire** and to preserve the privileged position of the Colbert clan, meant that Colbert was as much of a failure as a success. Even so, his partial failure should not detract from our assessment of him as one of the great figures of Louis XIV's reign. It is entirely characteristic of the politics of that era that when Colbert, undoubtedly the greatest administrator of the *ancien régime**, died, exhausted by work for his sovereign, neither Louis XIV nor his people regretted him.

The military reforms of Le Tellier and Louvois

It was during the first half of the reign of Louis XIV that Le Tellier, helped from 1662 by his son Louvois, transformed the army into a relatively well-organised instrument of war. Louis André pointed out in his excellent *Michel Le Tellier et Louvois* (**50**) that it is very hard to differentiate between the work of father and son, so closely did they cooperate. Both worked to reform the army, but from 1667 Louvois frequently accompanied the King to the armies or went alone to organise and inspect, making his presence felt and feared. This shared interest with the King, who loved military parades and warfare, and his utter devotion to the royal service, were responsible for the great confidence and friendship accorded Louvois, who entered the *Conseil d'en haut* in 1672. There, he was to develop a great influence over military affairs, the border provinces and foreign policy. After the death of Colbert, Louvois acquired the office of superintendant of buildings, in which role he tried to outdo his predecessor. The Le Tellier clan remained nearly as powerful as or more powerful than the Colbert clan in council and at court until his death at fifty in 1690. As Corvisier has recently shown, it is, however, a myth that Louvois ever became anything like an unofficial first minister (**51**).

Before Le Tellier's time, the army had been a collection of undisciplined, ill-fed and often infrequently paid private regiments and companies entirely dominated by the nobility. However, by the end of the first two decades of the personal rule an army had been created that was not only much larger, but was also largely in the hands of, and subordinated to the control of, the state. The reforms were numerous. Higher ranks were to be appointed on the basis of seniority rather than birth, the latter system having given rise to incompetence as well as quarrels and refusals to serve that prejudiced the service. The lot of the officer was improved in that proper pay was given, promotion prospects improved and pensions disbursed for those forced to retire. This attracted numerous rural nobles who had not been able to afford the costs of being a captain or a colonel under the old system, in which officers often had to provide for their own troops. Nevertheless, these ranks still remained venal*. Attempts were made to ensure less corruption and more regular pay for the soldiers, while the Invalides was built (1670–74) to house incapacitated old soldiers. The indiscipline of the soldiers was curbed by brutal punishments and the establishment of barracks in the frontier provinces with garrison towns; soldiers on the march were provided for by stocks along the way, which reduced their need to live by marauding even when on French territory. Modest reforms, therefore, were possible in the realm of discipline – but the passage of soldiers still terrified the local populations. Nor was it possible to exercise complete control over the officers. As Corvisier says, 'In spite of several decades of effort, Le Tellier and Louvois still had not succeeded in subjecting the nobility to the rules of strict obedience' (**51**, p. 332).

The structure of the army was reorganised too. Various services previously independent, such as the engineers and the artillery, were incorporated into the main structure. In the same spirit, the cavalry and the infantry were organised into proper regiments, with the grenadiers being formed in 1667 and the fusiliers in 1671. Smaller companies of only forty men were created, and formed into new battalions of fifteen companies, which made it easier for officers to discipline their men and harder for them to make a personal profit by declaring non-existent soldiers on the payroll. Equally important was the administrative organisation of the army, from inspection, training and equipment (uniforms were issued from the time of the Dutch War) to the preparation of supplies. The intendants* of the army, often personal clients of the Le Telliers, took on a greater role, but it was one which Louvois strictly supervised.

Recruitment was always hard except during famines such as those between 1693 and 1695, or in frontier provinces threatened by invasion. The establishment of the militia in 1688 ensured a fairer system than the passage of the recruiting sergeant. The effect of the reforms, in terms of size of the army that could be kept afoot, was considerable. It became possible to have a peace-time standing army of around 100,000 men. In wartime the size was much greater. There were 120,000 soldiers in 1672 and about 290,000 in 1688, including the rather ineffectual militias. The figure for 1703 may have risen as high as 400,000, although we must remain sceptical of this number. Nevertheless, it is clear that the combination of the reforms of Colbert with those of the two Le Telliers made possible the grandiose foreign policy that was based perhaps more on military strength than on sound diplomacy (**30**). It is to this diplomacy that we must turn if we are to understand the particular responsibility of Louis XIV in affairs of state.

4 Foreign Policy

Louis' first interest was foreign policy. It was traditionally the most noble of royal pursuits because it involved war, the defence of the commonwealth and the interests of the dynasty. Indeed, war was noble and glorious in itself and it was normal, there being no sound mechanisms for preserving peace. Foreign policy was therefore the field in which the King's aristocratic desire for *gloire** could best be expressed. *Gloire* itself can perhaps be translated as a reputation in the world and with posterity for nobility, honour and glorious feats of arms. That Louis was motivated by this desire has long been accepted. What is more doubtful is whether he aimed at either establishing universal monarchy for himself or natural frontiers for France. Although older textbooks may refer to these theories, the prevailing view today is that neither of these motives can explain his foreign policy. Gaston Zeller in the 1930s effectively demolished the natural frontiers thesis (**160**); the idea of universal monarchy was the understandable product of an influential pamphlet of 1667 and further anti-French propaganda written during the wars and widely circulated, but it was no more than a plausible indictment (**146**, chs. 1 and 2).

Serious historians of the period consider the most consistent thread to Louis' policy to have been the acquisition of defensible (rather than natural) frontiers. This aim is most clearly expressed in a famous letter by the military engineer Vauban to Louvois on 19 January 1673. 'Sire', he wrote, 'the King ought to think seriously about making his *pré carré* [perhaps: 'squaring off his frontiers']. This confusion of friendly and enemy places all mixed up together does not please me at all' (**219**, p. 73).

This *pré carré* was to be not so much a duelling field (which could be one meaning of the term) as a more linear frontier, without enclaves or 'gateways' giving easy access to the enemy, and defined by a line of impregnable fortresses. Vauban's meaning can be clearly understood by looking at a map of the eastern frontier. If the intention, revealed by the vague wording of the 1648 treaties, was to firm up the titles to Alsace, then the three bishoprics of Verdun, Toul and Metz, and the provinces of Alsace, Burgundy and Dauphiné were clearly all still vulnerable to attack from Luxembourg and Franche-Comté (still Spanish); and fortresses providing passage over the Rhine, like Strasbourg and Philippsburg, could be considered gateways to France for the imperial armies. Moreover, it seemed but a short step from Spanish Flanders through Picardy to the heart of France. Attempts to strengthen the frontier could be portrayed as defensive (Hatton in **146**), but we may note that Louis chose aggressive tactics to achieve his aim, even by the standards of the time. This entailed abandoning the strategy of Mazarin, who had been preparing the ground to exploit French preponderance by keeping a balance through negotiations, and by acquiring the expected compensations from the Spanish succession – and thereby achieving security by diplomatic means (**148**).

The prospect of acquiring the succession to the Spanish empire when its direct male line died out, as seemed imminent, has also been put forward as the focal point of Louis' foreign policy. Mazarin had cleverly married Louis to a daughter of Philip IV of Spain in 1660, knowing that her claim to the throne could not really be invalidated by any formal renunciation. It is true that the succession issue loomed large at certain moments – in 1668, and increasingly in the 1690s – but the indications are that Louis never expected to acquire the whole Spanish empire, and that the legacy of 1700 came as a complete surprise. Rather more realistically, he wished to ensure that he was in a sufficiently strong legal, diplomatic and military position to prevent Habsburg encirclement and have a real chance of gains by a partition with or without war. So it would probably be wrong to elevate the acquisition of the Spanish empire to the status of the prime motive of his policy before 1700. It is best seen as a thorny problem to be solved in the context of Louis' policy on defensible frontiers. This itself was to be achieved by imposing a French interpretation of the treaties of 1648 on the other states (**145**, ch. 9; **143**, **144**).

In spite of all the attempts by historians to impose, with the benefit of hindsight, a rational scheme on Louis' policy, the fact remains that it is extremely difficult to justify any single schema in detail. The present tendency is to emphasise the *ad hoc* nature of his policy in its details and even in the early major decisions, such as the Dutch War of 1672. These must also be explained in the context both of his personal psychology and his general maxims or assumptions. In the absence of a large and well-trained diplomatic corps with an efficient information-gathering service, Louis made sense of the world – and sometimes misinterpreted it – through a notion of 'true maxims' or true interests of states (**145**, ch. 2). It was for him a way of predicting their reactions in the light of their place in a natural order. This natural order envisaged absolute monarchy as the only respectable decision-making system, and he therefore found it hard to come to grips with the capacity of the parliamentary states to ignore previous treaties in the light of a new perspective or opinion, and he underestimated their determination. It was only late in his reign that he accorded the Maritime Powers the respect they deserved as important forces in the international order. He himself felt bound by honour, and by interest, as he was a legitimate sovereign, to adhere to treaties he had signed, unless some passably acceptable legal loophole could be found or the very fate of his own state seemed to depend upon breaking his word. His pessimistic view of human nature as expressed in his *Mémoires* led him to rely sometimes more on gratifications to foreign diplomats and rulers (**145**, ch. 5) than on careful attention to their interests.

What Lossky has called Louis' *a priori* reasoning derived, then, from his idea of true maxims and his vision of human nature, and consequently he made many mistakes – especially in the 1680s. He was a hard-working sovereign who read the dispatches carefully, but as Saint-Simon said, he had a mind '*au dessous du médiocre*'. At first his policy was characterised by a natural caution that was overwhelmed by youthful impetuosity and a desire to shine, but the hard lessons of experience gradually led him to moderate his ambitions and his tone. Nevertheless, in contrast to a Mazarin or a Richelieu, or even to his early ministers Lionne and Pomponne, Louis had not the capacity to conceptualise a system of relations that was far-sighted and sound (**152**). He thus autocratically imposed his own failings on his ministers in the first two decades, and from the 1680s chose men who reflected his own views. The result was a policy that led quickly to an apogee of *gloire** and hegemony in the 1680s (because after 1660 France really was the strongest single power in Europe), but it was one which succeeded in generating so much fear and hostility that the formation of a successful anti-French coalition was greatly facilitated. Even before he reached the height of his power, therefore, the King had already sown the seeds of discontent.

For Louis, Spain was still the main enemy of the early years. 'The state of the two crowns of France and of Spain is such today and has been for such a long time in the world that it is impossible to raise one without humbling the other' (**7**, p. 46). However, France needed time to recuperate after the long wars, and at first Mazarin's policy was continued. Spain was kept weak by France covertly helping Portugal to regain its freedom; England and the Dutch Republic were kept away from Spain with friendship and an alliance respectively; and the League of the Rhine, a grouping of north-west German states under French aegis, was maintained in order to isolate the Spanish Netherlands from Austria. The Emperor Leopold I was fully occupied with problems in Hungary and with the Turks and was keen to preserve peace in the West. Louis contented himself with establishing his reputation as a determined young sovereign by insisting on the rights of his ambassadors to precedence and, rather counterproductively, by being the only state to refuse to give the Roman authorities rights of police in the ambassadorial enclave; this had the effect of offending the Pope. In 1662 he purchased Dunkirk from a financially hard-pressed Charles II of England.

The Anglo-Dutch War of 1665–66 was an embarrassment to France, since it was bound by treaty to support the Dutch but wished to remain friends with England. Louis entered the war on the side of the Dutch in 1666 but managed to do nothing significant. The following year he fought his own first war against Spain in the Spanish Netherlands. The context was the death of Philip IV in 1665 and his will leaving his possessions to his son Carlos II and on his death to Philip's second daughter, from his second marriage. This ignored the rights of Louis' wife, Maria Theresa, the first daughter of Philip. Louis' official aim was to enforce a rather spurious claim to inherit these territories by virtue of a private law of devolution which gave primacy to children of first marriages. The argument was spurious because the law was private not dynastic, and because Carlos was still alive and so there was no question of either daughter yet having a real claim, but Spain was unprepared and French forces stronger. Louis led his armies on a military promenade during which place after place fell in quick succession.

The sudden war shocked England and the Dutch into peace and an alliance which Sweden joined in early 1668: the Triple Alliance. It was clear that extensive French gains could lead to a wider war and probable intervention by other states, so Louis invaded and took Franche-Comté as a bargaining counter and then acted as the very spirit of moderation. By the peace of Aix-la-Chapelle he settled for twelve towns in the Spanish Netherlands and gave back the rest of his conquests to Spain. His acquisitions left the Spanish Netherlands exposed to later attack, but the war had effectively ended Mazarin's system. Louis had perhaps never been very attached to that system, stemming from a man 'who loved me and whom I loved, who had rendered me great services, but whose ideas and manners were naturally quite different from mine' (**7**, p. 23). The League of the Rhine collapsed and Dutch fears were aroused: it had long been a Dutch maxim that France was a better friend than neighbour. England feared French expansionism (**144**).

A second reason for the end of the war was that Louis and Leopold had just agreed, in January 1668, a treaty of partition of the Spanish empire in the event of the death of the sickly boy Carlos II. In the light of the reluctance of his subjects to finance a war in 1667, Leopold chose the solution that went against his dynastic rights: partition. France was to get Naples and Sicily, along with Flanders, Franche-Comté and Navarre, while Austria would get Spain, the other Italian territories and most of the overseas empire. Louis had waged his short winter campaign to take Franche-Comté in order to force Spain in the ensuing peace to recognise the provisions of the partition treaty; only after Spain had done this did he agree to return the province. However, the partition treaty was never implemented because Carlos persisted in living, and because the French occupation of Lorraine in 1670 ruined the policy of *rapprochement* with the Emperor, since Austria was morally bound to defend Lorraine which was part of the Empire. Nevertheless, the partition treaty is good evidence of French territorial interests up to the end of the century.

The Dutch War

Although Louis claimed to make his own decisions, his natural caution and hesitancy led him to seek advice. Sonnino, in his painstaking investigations of the origins of the Dutch War of 1672, has shown that the factions and ministers surrounding the King did influence his decisions (**150**). For a long time historians felt that the war's origins lay in a combination of anger on the part of Louis at what he saw as Dutch arrogance in 1668, with the urgings of Colbert to diminish Dutch economic competition. This is only part of the story, which seems a little more complicated. It is true that Louis wanted a war at all costs and wanted his revenge on the

Dutch for abandoning him in 1668. Lionne was set to work to break up the Triple Alliance and secure the neutrality of the German states. The dominant influences on Louis were those of Marshal Turenne, bellicose and imprudent, whose weight worried the other ministers, and Louvois (**151**). Fearful for their own influence, the ministers played along with Louis and Turenne, and Le Tellier came around to supporting a war as it reflected and increased the influence of his son. Colbert, far from being the chief inspiration, was in favour of economy, but could not afford to be left out and so he quickly promised the necessary financial resources.

In keeping with such an imprudent policy, there were no proper war plans beyond attacking the Dutch in the hope either of quick concessions (which could hardly be strategically useful to France but might aid its commerce) or, and this was the real aim, of forcing Spain to join in. This would enable Louis to conquer the Spanish Netherlands legitimately. No thought was given to the probable consequences of such a conquest on the European system and no plan of campaign was drawn up for more than one year. In fact, the war was to drive the Dutch, France's one-time ally, into the arms of Spain and Austria and create the pattern of alliances for some time to come (**148, 149**).

After the end of the war Louis rewrote his memoirs in order to conceal all this and make it appear that he had been aiming at just what he got (**7, 146**, ch. 7). Even so, the war appears to have been the most serious mistake of his reign [**docs 33, 34**]. The campaign of 1672 was so successful that the Dutch had to open the dikes and flood their country to protect Amsterdam and gain time for other states to intervene. It destroyed the pro-French party in the Netherlands and propelled William of Orange to the head of the Republic. Subsequently, an anti-French coalition of Spain, Austria and the Dutch was formed in 1673. At this point, bowled over by his own triumphs, Louis rejected generous concessions from the Dutch and attacked the Spanish. In this way the war for personal glory in 1672 was transformed into a war in the interests of the French state in 1673, according to Ekberg. In his important study, Ekberg concludes that Louis 'had difficulty conceptualising a policy of state interest as a framework for his own actions', as he was unable to distinguish between his own desires and the good of the state (**152**, p. 182). Fortunately, some of his advisers could do so, like Courtin [**doc. 34**] and Pomponne, Louis' new minister for foreign affairs. The war became more general and finally, after

1677, French strength began to tell. Not that France was without difficulties; on the contrary, like the other belligerents, France found itself unable to pay for a long war. The extraordinary fiscal measures destroyed most of Colbert's reforms and provoked peasant revolts in 1674 and 1675. Peace negotiations began in 1676, but 1677 and 1678 saw French victories which improved Louis' negotiating position.

The Peace of Nymegen (1678–79) accorded France some fortresses in the Spanish Netherlands and the whole province of Franche-Comté (**144**). The Peace can be presented as a triumph for France, as a moderate settlement after French victories over the rest of Europe; or it can be seen as a compromise Peace which retained what France could defend after the trials of a long war (**159**). The Peace was negotiated by Pomponne, Louis' moderate minister, who had a wider and sounder vision of European affairs than Louis himself. According to Sonnino, the dismissal of Pomponne in 1679 resulted from the King's feeling that he had 'won the war and lost the peace'. While it is true that Louis learned some lessons from the war, especially about Dutch power being sufficient to prevent him annexing the Spanish Netherlands, it appears also to have increased his arrogance and his dominance over his own council.

The reunions

These attitudes characterise the next ten years, which are regarded as the apogee of French power. In internal policy this was the period of persecution of the Huguenots and heightened conflict with the Pope. In his foreign policy, the King chose to exploit his position by rounding out his frontiers a little more and strengthening his grip on disputed territories. The peacetime strength of the army was 140,000 men, an enormous burden on the finances: foreign policy was influenced by the legal expertise of Colbert's brother, Colbert de Croissy, who had replaced Pomponne, and by the unsubtle Louvois, whose influence with Louis was at its height. The emphasis was on force and opportunism; little attention was paid to the European effects of French actions. Thus we see the policy of forceful 'reunions' of 1679–84. Special courts were set up, *chambres de réunion*, which were intended to provide the legal basis for the annexation of the dependencies of territories gained by France in 1648. Of course, such tactics were not new in international relations, as states would usually exploit the vagueness of treaties. On the other hand, the French reunions were particularly extensive and systematic (**146**, ch. 3).

Numerous territories down the eastern border of France, from the Spanish Netherlands to Lorraine, were annexed on various feudal pretexts. Vauban constructed fortifications in the strategically important areas, building a line of fortresses along the frontier from the Netherlands to Alsace. There was no legal claim to Strasbourg, but it was intimidated into surrender in September 1681, as it controlled a vital crossing of the Rhine. At the same time the fortress of Casale in northern Italy was occupied after purchase. This city was strategically important because it checked potential aggression by the Duchy of Savoy – and greatly offended this ally. Luxembourg was blockaded from November 1681.

Although there were protests, the French army was too powerful for others to risk intervention. Some of the German princes were bought off with subsidies – like the Elector of Brandenburg – while the Emperor was preoccupied by the Turkish threat. Louis even told the Sultan that he would not intervene against him, thus profiting from the Turkish attack on the Christian Empire. When the Turks were forced to abandon the siege of Vienna in 1683, Spain felt secure enough to declare war on France, to try to prevent the loss of Luxembourg – but no other powers joined in and Luxembourg was quickly lost. The Truce of Ratisbon, in 1684, arranged with the mediation of the Emperor, recognised for twenty years the French gains made by the reunions and in the war.

The Nine Years War

Having had to stand by and watch Louis seize various territories, powerless as they had been to intervene, the other statesmen of Europe were worried. They began to make diplomatic alliances to guarantee the Truce of Ratisbon, in order thereby to discourage further French expansion. Thereafter, Louis would have liked to have been able to convert the Truce into an agreed treaty, but he had little chance of this. The inspiring Austrian victories over the Turks not only strengthened the Emperor's prestige in Germany but also raised hopes that he would soon turn his victorious armies against the French. Furthermore, Louis' failure to help defeat the Turks had cost him the aura of defender of Christendom and Catholicism. The French revocation of the Edict of Nantes in 1685 (which may well have been influenced by the

evident need to prove Louis' Catholic credentials) frightened the
Protestant states and greatly eased William of Orange's task of
building a coalition against France. Louis and Louvois could
perceive the mounting danger to the eastern frontier and quick-
ened the pace of the programme of fortifications designed by
Vauban (**148**).

The frontier in Alsace was still weak because it lay open to attack
from Philippsburg, in the Palatinate, and from the Electorate of
Cologne. The latter should not normally have posed a problem,
since another French client was expected to succeed to the
existing Francophile archbishop. However, instead of ratifying the
election of Cardinal von Fürstenberg, which was contested by the
Emperor, the Pope – who was offended by the French pressure on
him and by a dispute over the French church – opted for the
Emperor's candidate. This diplomatic defeat was in August 1688,
and in September French troops invaded both the Palatinate and
Cologne, which was threatened by the army gathered by William of
Orange. Taking advantage of the French attack on the Rhineland,
which left the Netherlands temporarily safe, William invaded
England in November. By May 1689 he was King of England and
therefore able to fulfil his dream of creating a European coalition
against Louis, the aims of which were to reduce France to the
frontiers of 1659. The French devastation of the Palatinate over
the winter, a strategy designed to deprive the enemy of supplies
and to terrorise the opposition, appalled the German states and
alienated them still further. What had begun in the French estimation as a limited campaign to seize strategically important territories and encourage the Turks to go on fighting ended up being a
major European war (**146**, ch. 8).

The Nine Years War, or the War of the League of Augsburg
(1688–97), was the result of twenty years of French aggression.
France, isolated and unprepared, was now faced with the full range
of European states. Lossky sees this situation as the result of
incoherent policies: France had abandoned the security of a sound
system of alliances for quick victories, yet from 1685 had paradoxically been trying to build up a pro-French party in Spain with a
view to the Spanish succession, which implied a more friendly
policy towards the Spanish Netherlands. Is this evident confusion
or a case of keeping two irons in the fire at once? Certainly, the
scale of the war took Louis by surprise, and it is hard to avoid the
conclusion that it was the product of poor and overconfident
policies:

In the War of Devolution and the Dutch War Louis had already destroyed the Rhine League buffer beyond any hope of resurrection. Now, in the 1680s most of the rest of France's alliance system was dismantled, not by design, but through negligence. (**148**, p. 178)

Sonnino feels that Louis soon came to recognise his mistakes, but emphasises that the pre-emptive strike of 1688 was a recurrent characteristic of a man who remained essentially similar in approach over the years (**149**).

The war required a defensive strategy from France on land, and most of the fighting was in the form of sieges and of battles that could not be followed up because of enemy fortresses. Each side had about 220,000 troops but France had the advantage of internal communications. In 1689 and 1690 it had seemed as if Colbert's naval policy would pay off, with a likely invasion of England. A victory which gave France command of the English Channel was won off Beachy Head in 1690, but in May 1692 the situation was reversed by the Anglo-Dutch naval victory of La Hogue. Louis then allowed the navy to decline and the privateering war to escalate, which brought important profits to French seaports and severely damaged allied trade (**181–2**).

By 1693 it had become clear to both William and Louis that neither side could win outright. After the death of Louvois in 1691, Pomponne was recalled and a more sophisticated diplomacy undertaken, with negotiations from 1692 aimed at breaking up the Grand Alliance. These finally bore fruit in 1696, when Victor Amadeus II of Savoy was detached from the Grand Alliance by France giving up its Italian policy and buying him off with the fortress of Pignerol for Savoy, at the same time as Casale was given back to Mantua. This was the end of two centuries of French ambitions to Italy, but it was the price to be paid for concentrating on the northern frontier (**146**, ch. 10).

Unable to win, and hard-pressed to raise sufficient war finance, Louis was now prepared to offer terms that would suit the English and the Dutch, who were also anxious to end the war. Although the Emperor made more difficulties, he could not refuse the French terms when abandoned by his allies. Serious negotiations began in May 1697 and were concluded in the autumn with the Peace of Ryswick. Louis recognised William as the legitimate ruler of Britain and conceded defeat over the Palatinate and the Electorate of Cologne. Of his gains since 1679 he kept only

Strasbourg and Alsace and surrendered the rest. The Peace made it plain that there were limits to French power. France sorely needed peace in 1697, for the fiscal system had developed all the old abuses, new taxes had been imposed, and the peasantry was sinking into deeper poverty during the agricultural depression. Yet war was to break out again only four years later.

The War of the Spanish Succession

Neither Louis XIV nor William III wanted a war over the Spanish succession. From the spring to the autumn of 1698 Louis and William were engaged in negotiating the First Partition Treaty. By this arrangement the main part of the Spanish inheritance would go to the Wittelsbach prince, the Elector of Bavaria. The Italian possessions would be divided between France and Austria, in the persons of the second son of Emperor Leopold and the Dauphin*. Although the Spanish and Austrian courts were outraged by the proposals, there was a good chance that the arrangement could have been imposed upon them by concerted action. Being neither a Bourbon nor an Austrian Habsburg, Joseph Ferdinand, the Elector of Bavaria, was a good compromise candidate. When Carlos actually decided to make his will in favour of the Elector, in order to preserve the Spanish empire complete, it seemed as if peace too might be preserved. Tragically, the Elector died early in 1699. There being no candidate with a respectable claim who was not either a Bourbon or an Austrian Habsburg, the chances of peace died with him.

Nevertheless, a Second Partition Treaty was negotiated by the same powers by March 1700. It was based on the first, in that a son of the Emperor who was unlikely to inherit the Empire, the Habsburg Archduke Charles, was to be given the Elector's portion, with the exception of the Milanais which was to be added to that of the Dauphin*. The partition would probably not have stood the test of time, because it tried to reconcile too many conflicting interests. The Maritime Powers would refuse to let France acquire the Spanish Netherlands, and Louis could appreciate this position. But if France was to get anything out of the Partition, it would have to be in Spain itself or in Italy. Spain was out of the question, as any extension of French power there would create a huge and effective Bourbon bloc, one that could not be resisted. So Spain had to go to the Habsburgs. Louis therefore concentrated on preventing a juncture of the Habsburg domains by interposing himself in Italy, in Milan: this would separate the Habsburg family bloc of territories. But the Emperor was unlikely to agree to renounce the advantages of the inheritance and was reluctant to give up his recent Italian ambitions. He may have been realistic enough to know that he could not have everything, but he did want part of Italy. An impasse was therefore inevitable; the various interests were simply too diverse to be reconciled (**156; 146**, ch. 2).

In the event, Carlos II put the chimera of keeping the Spanish empire intact above all other considerations. For this reason he willed it to the candidate most likely to preserve its integrity. A glimmer of hope lay in the fact that it was not the Dauphin* he chose, but Philippe, great-grandson of Louis, who seemed unlikely to become King of France. On 9 November 1700 a courier arrived at Fontainebleau bearing news of the will. A council meeting was held to debate the best course of action. The ministers were split on whether to accept the testament or to implement the Partition Treaty. The next day a second meeting was held under pressure from the arrival of the official Spanish courier who had instructions to move on to Vienna to offer the crown to Archduke Charles in the event of a French refusal (**149**). Sensing that Louis was himself inclined to accept the will, his minister Torcy moderated his opposition, and the sense of the meeting was for acceptance (**10**).

In Louis' estimation of the situation, war was almost inevitable. He therefore decided not to woo the Maritime Powers into helping him fight the Emperor. Instead, to improve his defensive position, he occupied by surprise fortresses in the Spanish Netherlands. Austrian troops attacked the Milanais in March 1701, and by September 1701 a Grand Alliance had been formed against France. The war was in full swing in the summer of 1702.

There remain a number of imponderables about the origins of the war. It is hard to disentangle from the complex chain of events those causes that lay in the nature of the international system and the general presuppositions about normal behaviour, from those that relate to the particular responsibility of individuals. Was Louis right to station troops in the Spanish Netherlands in 1701, even though this provoked William III into war? After all, if war was already inevitable, then Louis' step was a reasonable defensive measure. If on the other hand there were still chances for peace, then Louis seriously misjudged the situation.

Even so, it may be that the 'blame' lies in the nature of the system by which each side, through poor communications and lack of common negotiations (which usually only took place after wars), failed to communicate its true thinking to the other parties. It would be centuries before it became clear that secret clauses and secret treaties served to increase the risks of war rather than simply protect a state in the event of war. That there could be a balance of power between states was an idea that was only just emerging, largely as a result of these conflicts.

Statesmen still conceived of international relations as essentially a competitive arena in which the rise of one state inevitably involved the decline of another; they thought also of foreign affairs as the arena for aristocratic values of military prowess and virtue. Rulers thought primarily in dynastic terms, and concern for their subjects was more of a conventional platitude in their Christian discourse than it was a true feeling of compassion. Hence war was a frequent and, within their mentality, a natural recourse, a surer response to circumstances than negotiations. The fear of universal monarchy that the prestige policies of Louis had generated was not a negligible factor. Above all, a more detailed analysis of the negotiations and actions of the various parties reveals that mutual mistrust was a major factor, since all those who were involved refused to interpret the others at face value (**156**).

Certainly, William and Louis had wanted peace in 1698–1700. That being so, are we to blame the Emperor for his determination to fight France in order to wrest concessions from Louis, since it was the premonition of this decision that led Louis to take pre-emptive action? In historical context we might observe that in the circumstances of late 1700 – after Philip V had been proclaimed King of Spain – no ruler would expect another one to surrender a part of his territory simply because he was likely to lose it in war. A similar difficulty lies in estimating the effect of Spanish policy. In many ways the legacy to France was bound to provoke Austria to war – the Emperor had recognised this in 1668 by negotiating a partition and so too had William and Louis in 1698. The major protagonists thus seemed aware that in the end, with or without war, a partition was inevitable. Why then did Carlos and his advisers attempt the impossible by aiming to keep the Spanish empire intact in the hands of a single ruler? One reason is pressure from within Spain, where the elite was not prepared to stand by and see it dismembered (**145**, ch. 9).

The historian may be forgiven for believing that ultimately these threads of explanation cannot be woven into a satisfactory whole. What is needed is a hierarchy of levels of explanation, which would begin perhaps with the system itself, then go on to relate to this not just the individual policies but also the assessment of them by other actors in the scene. Too many factors of different orders of importance discourage any tendency to apportion blame, but awareness of them increases understanding.

The war was to be long and extremely arduous. It brought in its train increased taxes and the extension to their very limits of every abuse that could be practised in the financial system. It brought France to the brink of disaster.

On the face of it, France was in a strong position with a large army, internal lines of communication and possession of most of the disputed territories. Important allies were Savoy and Bavaria, each with a good army. However, the Grand Alliance benefited enormously from the financial strength of the Netherlands and especially of Britain. The Maritime Powers were able to subsidise the allied cause with sufficient funds to keep large armies of German troops in the field. These were commanded by two particularly brilliant generals, Marlborough and Prince Eugen. There were four main fronts in the war, and by early 1709 France had lost on all of them. This time, battles, rather than sieges, were to decide the outcome. In 1703 Victor Emmanuel of Savoy joined the Alliance, ultimately putting at risk the French position in Italy, though at first he lost to them. In 1704 Marlborough and Eugen won the important battle of Blenheim, which led to the Allied occupation of Bavaria and the loss of the German fortresses by France. In 1705, France held the line in the Netherlands and Italy but lost Catalonia. The year 1706 was decisive as Marlborough's victory at Ramillies led to the overrunning of the Spanish Netherlands. This in turn forced an end to the French campaign in south Germany. In Italy troops were recalled, but in September Eugen defeated the French at Turin and the army had to retreat across the Alps. Louis began to offer terms to the Allies but they were unable to agree amongst themselves. France was by no means defeated and held ground in 1707. The French defeat at Oudenarde in 1708 opened the whole of northern France to invasion. Lille, the last major bastion in Flanders, fell in December of that year.

France was in desperate straits, its finances seemed utterly exhausted and Louis was prepared to make peace. He acceded to all the Allied demands except to help in the removal of Philip V from the throne of Spain, where the Bourbon King was now popular. That is to say, Louis was ready to give up the Spanish empire as long as his honour was saved. The Allied insistence on this clause led Louis to break off negotiations and appeal to his people for one more effort. This enabled France to survive 1709 and 1710, by which time changes in British politics had led to separate peace negotiations with Torcy. In effect, Britain deserted its allies, secured a settlement for itself and forced its partners to the conference table. The death of the Emperor and the succession to the imperial throne of the former Archduke Charles removed an obstacle to peace: there was little point in the Dutch fighting to recreate the Empire of Charles V. The victory by the French under Marshal Villars at Denain in 1712 proved that the Dutch and the Austrians could not go it alone. By 1713 the Peace of Utrecht had been negotiated, and in 1714 it was followed by that of Rasdadt with the Emperor.

The peace treaties left French borders pretty much as they had been in 1697 after Ryswick. At the end of Louis' reign, therefore, France had succeeded in imposing its own interpretation of the Peace of Westphalia on Europe, including the confirmation of Alsace, and had kept the parts of Flanders and the province of Franche-Comté that it had seized. A defensible frontier had been constructed. Nevertheless, the cost had been terribly high not just in physical terms – the hardship and suffering of war with its financial exactions – but also in terms of the international position of France. In 1661 France had been the arbiter of Europe, but in 1715 a peace had been imposed upon it by a powerful alliance. If the war appeared to confirm a territorial *status quo* for France, the gains of the War of the Spanish Succession were meagre indeed. The Spanish empire was dismembered and the Bourbon presence in Spain rendered nearly impotent.

A measure of the real changes that had come about is the fact that England and Austria were the true beneficiaries of the Peace. They had risen to be major powers in their own right, and in rising they had altered the balance and checked the potential for French hegemony (**144**). That Louis XIV failed to recognise the trend of events and to respond effectively is perhaps a major criticism of his policies. Of course, some aspects of the changes were well beyond his control. In Germany the traditional policy of French support for a German league in defence of liberties against the Emperor was hindered by the development of the autonomy of the states, as well as by the decline in importance of religious divisions (**146**, ch. 9). The cyclical depression in European, and therefore also French, agriculture set new limits to the military capacity of France for fiscal reasons.

So strong is the myth generated by Louis' grandiose domestic style that criticism of his foreign policy may sound heretical. And yet, it was a significant failing of Louis that he remained so much a man of his own generation, a man so deeply rooted in conceptions of absolute monarchy, that he failed to comprehend the changes that were occurring in the world system. For much of his reign it is difficult to detect any long-term view of the European system, and Louis' pursuit of French and his own dynastic territorial interests smacks of an opportunism that was saved from disaster only by French military strength. This strength was undermined by the advances of the Dutch and Austrian armies by the 1680s. Thus, even if we were able to arrive at a more sympathetic understanding of Louis' policies in the light of research on the period, we may still criticise the lack of a flexibility in conceptions, even his apparent inability to conceptualise the changes. The King's limitations in this respect had wider consequences. Louis more or less knowingly chose to put foreign policy before policies of reform and in each crisis chose the route of authority rather than consultation in domestic affairs. Trade was sacrificed to military ventures, and sound finance sacrificed to the needs of the moment. By 1715, France was an exhausted giant with feet of clay.

5   Church and State

During the reign of Louis XIV, religion was still a vital issue. It was the King's right and duty to direct affairs of religion in France, and therefore to govern relations between church and state. However, it would be misleading to imply too sharp a distinction between the two sets of institutions. Although church and state existed in a separate form in this period, it is important to realise that their degree of interpenetration was high. Each was, so to speak, a part of the other, and depended on the other. The monarchy was still theocratic, for royal power was believed to derive from God, and the King was widely believed to have something of the divine in him, conferred by his anointing at the time of his coronation. The ceremony at Reims confirmed this link in a traditional form that was believed to go back to Hugues Capet. The crowds that flocked to be cured of scrofula by the royal touch testify to this belief among the people, as does the assumption that the King could do no wrong (unlike his evil ministers!). The King thus had a divine right to rule, a right Louis firmly believed in. Disobedience to the King, God's lieutenant on earth, was nothing less than sacrilegious. The church was therefore the strongest of moral and ideological supports for the monarchy. Both institutions shared a profound preoccupation with hierarchy and order (**20**, chs. 2 and 3).

The administrative structure of the state reflected this relationship. Royal administrative circumscriptions were loosely based on ecclesiastical divisions, from parishes to bishoprics and archbishoprics, although boundaries rarely coincided exactly. By the late seventeenth century the concordance was at its most exact at the level of the parishes, which usually formed the basis of the tax communities. The crown made use of the priests and bishops to inform the population of laws and victories, and bishops often played an important role in aspects of local government. They were expected to support the demands of the crown in the meetings of provincial estates, where they had a significant number of deputies [**doc. 28**]. Furthermore, the Assembly of Clergy, which met every

five years, was obliged to grant a 'free gift' of several million *livres**
to the monarchy. Even in wartime, the monarchy never succeeded
in taxing church wealth at a high rate, but it did devise almost as
good a system, that of loans raised on the credit of the church –
loans that mounted up without being repaid.

However, ecclesiastical structures still retained an independent
jurisdiction, justified by the spiritual role of the church in society
in contrast to the essentially temporal power of the King. Yet the
boundary between the spiritual and the temporal spheres was hard
to draw exactly. While the respective roles had been defined by the
Concordat of Bologna (1516), and while the King insisted on
overall supremacy in the courts, to be exerted through his
parlement* of Paris, numerous conflicts of jurisdiction still arose.
In order to understand the twists and turns of ecclesiastical affairs,
it is important to comprehend the mentality of the time which
thought so much in terms of jurisdiction. Indeed, although important differences of theology did exist between the churches and
within the Catholic church, as we shall see, it is helpful to view
many aspects of clerical–secular relations in terms of legal rights
and privileges*. The church had temporal powers and was a
corporation in society, and so too were the royal courts. In the
*ancien régime** all courts and institutions were jealous of their
powers and privileges and sought to extend them whenever
possible. A case fought and won would serve as a useful precedent
on the next occasion. Thus, even in an age of undeniable spiritual
reform, most theological issues took on a jurisdictional air.

Examples are easy to find. In general, the monarchy was anxious
to extend its jurisdiction over the institutions of the church and to
reject papal interference – without going so far as to break with
Rome. However, when persecuted by the state, bishops, even
Jansenist bishops and *curés*, could appeal to Rome as a higher jurisdiction. On the other hand, when the Pope sided with the King,
the same Jansenists could appeal to a council of the church as
being above the Pope (**169**). On a more prosaic level, Jesuits who
had been granted powers in the localities were sometimes opposed
by the existing church authorities, and preachers of one religious
order might receive no cooperation from the local establishments
of another when performing missionary work. There were conflicts
between church courts and the Paris parlement*, which was always
happy to exploit its privilege of accepting appeals *comme d'abus*
(against abuses of church justice) by overturning verdicts reached
in the church courts. Confusing as these permutations may be,

they are an important facet of the relationship between church and state and figure in all the major conflicts of the era.

The temporal power of the church was indeed considerable. It was a great landowner, with huge revenues from rents, seigneurial* dues and clerical tithes. Many bishoprics or abbeys had an income of 10,000 *livres** or considerably more (30–40,000 *livres*) while others enjoyed literally princely revenues. The abbey of Saint-Germain-des-Prés was the richest living with 250,000 *livres* a year (**176**). Part of these revenues went towards the upkeep of the church as an institution for the saving of souls. But most of the money went to the bishops and abbots, who often lived in the style of aristocrats. This is hardly surprising, since about 90 per cent of them were indeed aristocrats by birth! Church benefices therefore served as an immense source of royal patronage for the sons and daughters of the *noblesse*. Many ecclesiastical incomes even had charges drawn on them from pensions granted to non-clericals. Pensions and sees alike would be solicited at court, since they came within the sphere of the King's prerogative. The King found it convenient to confer politically sensitive sees on members of loyal families like the Colberts or the Le Telliers; other sees would go to the sons of the influential higher nobility, like the Noailles and the Villeroys, which liked to place one son in the church while others acquired governorships or went into the army (**35**). Given the importance of patronage and the court in the system of government, we must recognise that in this sphere also the church was inextricably bound up with the state. The higher clergy contributed thus to the compromise between crown and nobility that was a feature of the reign of Louis XIV.

Both the Protestant and the Catholic churches had experienced considerable changes since the end of the Wars of Religion. The two churches continued to have a legal existence in France, since the Huguenot church had been protected by the Edict of Nantes of 1598. However, the position of the Huguenots was affected by Cardinal de Richelieu's successful policy in the 1620s of breaking their military power (and therefore that of the Protestant magnates, their leaders) by destroying their fortresses. Whatever the frictions between Protestants and Catholics in the localities, by mid-century the Protestant community was entirely loyal to the crown. It was a community, no longer dangerous, whose numbers were in slow decline. Yet its very existence seemed anomalous in an age when religious toleration was not a principle but a political expedient granted out of weakness (**163**; **44**, ch. 8).

In contrast, for the Catholic church, the seventeenth century was a period of dynamism. The Catholic Reformation set in motion by the Council of Trent was well under way, rectifying the kinds of abuses that had done so much to generate early Protestantism. The Catholic renewal had a real effect upon the clergy. By the 1660s they were better trained and considerably more moral and conscientious, and numerous religious communities had been set up both for preaching the Gospel to the 'pagan' peasantry and for charitable works. The first half of the century had been the age of committed, saintly ecclesiastics like Bérulle, Vincent de Paul and François de Sales, who all exerted a profound influence on subsequent generations. The reforms in the dioceses, too, were beginning to have a noticeable effect upon the laity, which was being encouraged, even forced, to conform to new religious practices (**161, 29, 177**).

Historians such as Jean Delumeau have pointed out that in many ways the two religions were actually attempting the same difficult task of Christianising the people of Europe (**161**). Both were intent upon stamping out magical beliefs and on inculcating a more learned notion of Christianity, one that emphasised internal moral and religious precepts rather than outward conformity. They diverged of course on vital questions of theology; but seen from below, from the point of view of the common people, the choice of religion was often much less about these issues of theology than about social networks, family values and traditional influences. The policy of Louis towards the Huguenots must therefore be interpreted in the context of changing structures and attitudes not just in the Protestant community but also in the Catholic one. Reformed Catholicism had a missionary zeal which led it to regard Protestantism not only as a theological affront but also as unnecessary, since it had grown out of criticism of abuses which were no longer existent. Many Catholics thought that the way was now open to reuniting the Christian church (**165**).

However, the Catholic church was not without its own internal conflicts. In this great age of debate and of practical attempts at renewal, all was in movement. The Society of Jesus was increasingly influential in ecclesiastical politics, especially because the King's confessors were Jesuit, and because the *Dévôt* Party* was strong at court. Even so, the Jesuits aroused much opposition for their casuistry, which to many implied an emphasis upon outward conformity, rather than a stricter inner faith which they believed had been essential to the primitive church. Amongst their

77

opponents, the Jansenists represented the strictest form of Catholicism, pessimistic about human nature, profoundly influenced by the writings of St Augustine, and uncompromising on the thorny issue of grace and free will: although they stopped short of accepting the Calvinist doctrine of predestination, they nevertheless believed that not everyone had been blessed with efficacious grace, and that therefore only some could be saved. This led to a very personal, inward-looking religion amongst the Jansenists. The independence inherent in the Jansenist theology inspired exaggerated fears on the part of Richelieu and the *Dévôts*. The spirit of opposition displayed by some Jansenists during the *Frondes** led Mazarin towards a policy of persecution from 1656. It is clear that this division between Catholics, in the context of a religious renewal, was a complicated political legacy to Louis (**169**).

Other problems were to prove almost as difficult. If the Jesuits were proponents of papal authority, there was nevertheless in France a strong sense of independence from Rome, known to historians as Gallicanism. The monarchy generally encouraged this sentiment because it buttressed royal freedom of action. Gallicanism appealed to much of the clergy at all levels, and especially to the Sorbonne, and took on a different connotation according to the milieu. The Paris parlement*, as the royal law court, naturally exerted its influence against Rome, and was prepared to interfere in church affairs in the hope of expanding its jurisdiction. (A major theme of the eighteenth century was to be the support the Jansenists found in the parlement against the hostile combination of King and bishops.) Gallican bishops might resist royal and *parlementaire* interference, pursuing their own anti-papal line, but they would be loath to anger Rome too much because the Papacy upheld their place in the ecclesiastical hierarchy. This place was being increasingly challenged by Richerism, a movement amongst parish priests (*curés*) that emphasised their independent role in the church, rather than their subordination to the bishops. Faced with these movements, royal Gallicanism, as we shall see, was much more an affair of circumstances, as the King tried to navigate between these various shoals. Difficulties were to arise when the King wished to alter his attitude to Rome, for political reasons. His own courts and the university were prepared to uphold his original policy, even though the King had abandoned it. They insisted, rather contentiously from the King's point of view, that France had fundamental laws that even the King could not alter (**172**).

All of the issues faced by Louis XIV therefore pre-dated his reign and reflect longer-term problems. Royal policies were not static, but changed in response to altered circumstances within the churches in France. To deal with Gallicanism first of all, Louis' assumptions about his own majesty and grandeur led him into an injudicious conflict with the Pope over the *régale*, which was the right possessed by the monarchy to receive the revenues of church sees while they remained vacant. It was a right long recognised in northern France, but it was extended, by fiscal edicts of 1673 and 1675, to southern sees. Two Jansenist bishops who protested were condemned by their archbishop and one of them appealed to Rome. Pope Innocent XI (1676–89), who was both pro-Jansenist and an intransigent defender of papal rights, excommunicated the archbishop and criticised royal policy (**174**).

Louis responded by mobilising a special session of the Assembly of the Clergy, packed with sympathetic bishops, to challenge papal claims. In 1682 this assembly promulgated Four Articles (in **15**) which summarised the Gallican position of the French church, and ordered that they be taught in the university and regarded as a part of French law. Innocent replied by refusing to invest bishops appointed to sees by the crown, with the result that thirty-five dioceses soon lacked episcopal direction. In 1687 the French ambassador in Rome was excommunicated, and in 1688 Louis was resoundingly defeated by the Pope in his project to have a client elected to the strategically important see of Cologne. Louis occupied the papal enclave of Avignon, but his serious problems in foreign policy and his growing piety prompted him to take advantage of a new, more tractable Pope, to reach a diplomatic compromise that smacked of capitulation. The upshot was that the Four Articles would no longer be taught – though Louis could not prevent the parlement* from continuing to uphold them – while the Pope would invest the royally appointed bishops provided that revenues collected in the interim were paid over to the diocese. The affair was fully concluded by the Pacification of 1693 and the highly orthodox Declaration of 1695, by which Louis gave bishops greater jurisdiction over the clergy within their sees. Avignon was given back and the diplomatic franchises in Rome conceded – and the secret excommunication of Louis annulled. The King had finally come down on the side of traditional hierarchical values (**41**, ch. 7).

It is clear from the evolution of this rather pointless conflict that Louis had gravely underestimated the power of the Papacy. His overconfident attitude towards the Papacy, analysed by Sonnino for the 1660s, thus appears to have lasted until the 1690s (**173**). From that date Louis' policy, reinforced by the Jesuitism of his confessor, veered towards a *rapprochement* with Rome and became almost anti-Gallican. In this later period of his reign, Louis was to exploit his accommodation with Rome to bring to a head his condemnation of the Quietists and his persecution of the Jansenists. The Declaration of 1695 has rarely been appreciated for what it was: namely, the new legal basis of support for the episcopal hierarchy, in alliance with the crown, against the members of the lower clergy, who were by then widely influenced by Richerism and Jansenism.

At the height of the quarrel with Rome, and just when he had refused to help Christian Europe to defeat the Turkish invasion, Louis chose to revoke the Edict of Nantes. No doubt he calculated that the timing was good for his rather ragged Catholic credentials. Historians are also agreed that through Madame de Maintenon he had found a new sense of piety which was reflected in his personal conduct. But the Revocation of 1685 had much longer-term origins. In a sense, as Orcibal has shown, it was envisaged from 1598 and the Edict of Nantes itself. The Edict of Nantes was a temporary expedient that had, so to speak, become semi-permanent, simply because a *coup de force* was deemed unwise (especially in wartime), and because a policy of progressive legal restrictions on Protestants in the state seemed to be working. Such had been Richelieu's policy, followed also by Mazarin, who only back-tracked from 1652 to 1656 as a result of the *Frondes** (**164**; **44**, ch. 8).

From 1661 Louis determined to confine the Protestants ever more closely within the original limits imposed by the Edict of Nantes. Thus, everywhere that new churches had been built they were destroyed, to the extent that about half of the existing Huguenot churches were pulled down from 1663 to 1665. Restrictions were placed on Protestant pastors, preventing them from visiting the dying in hospitals, for example, or teaching in schools, and from 1663 no more conversions to Protestantism were to be legally permitted. Economic and administrative restrictions were imposed on practising Huguenots, making their life more difficult, and fiscal and financial incentives were given to those who converted to Catholicism (**167**, ch. 5). At this stage there was no project to revoke the Edict; it was more a question of making its revocation unnecessary. Louis felt keenly his role as king of an ordered society, and the existence of two faiths was naturally anomalous for His Most Christian Majesty.

The Dutch War led to a relaxation of the repressive policy, but after the Peace of Nymegen Louis was more confident than ever in his role as absolute monarch. The measures taken to destroy rural Huguenot churches had left thousands without the formal exercise of any religion. They were outside any parish, any cadre – and this was worrying for the *ancien régime** mind – and unable to have access to the proper rituals of birth, marriage and death. It was widely thought that a little pressure would bring them back to the fold (**166**). Civil persecution was therefore renewed with redoubled vigour, and the first *dragonnades** took place in Poitou in 1681. The 30,000 or so conversions resulting from this billeting of violent soldiers in Protestant communities were certainly numerically impressive. The state's methods encouraged Catholics to increase their own local violence. The year 1683 saw extensive *dragonnades*, 1684 the same, and in the first months of 1685 some 300–400,000 conversions took place. 'The dragoons have been excellent missionaries,' wrote Madame de Sévigné to Bussy Rabutin (**12**, 28 Oct. 1685). Many historians have asserted that Louis never approved this policy, but this is a partisan defence: it is not credible that Louis was ignorant of the extent of the violence. Louis seems to have worked on the assumption that the large number of conversions had undermined the *raison d'être* of the Edict of Nantes. Therefore, on 17 October 1685, he revoked it by issuing the Edict of Fontainebleau.

Historians now agree that the decision for the Revocation was made by Louis. However, the responsibility was not his alone, and recent research has revealed the importance of the underlying assumptions of the Catholic divines. The King was certainly under constant pressure from his entourage to remedy the 'scandal' of Protestantism. Violence was held to be an acceptable remedy because Catholics regarded Protestantism as an aggressive heresy against which Catholic souls must be protected. According to Dompnier, who has studied the Catholic views in writings and sermons, Protestantism was seen as the exact negative of Catholicism, and not as a religion possessing its own integrity. Therefore, by destroying churches and preventing pastors from preaching, it should theoretically be possible fatally to undermine the basis of authority which they supposed the faith rested upon (**162**). This failure to see Protestantism for what it was, was a major mistake, because Protestantism was not a faith dependent upon pastors for its inculcation. It had been internalised, and was grounded in individual consciences. The circular letter of the Assembly of the Clergy of 1682 is a perfect illustration of this misunderstanding:

> We pray for them, even though they curse us, and however much evil they might do us, we want to employ all possible means to procure their well-being, and the greatest ... which is to say their conversion and the salvation of their souls.

The news of the Revocation was greeted with joy by almost all Catholics – the Pope, however, was reserved and lukewarm in his congratulations – while distinguished bishops like Bossuet, Fléchier and Fénelon all took part in the vast missionary movement that gathered pace. Yet, as is well known, the Edict of Fontainebleau proved to be a bad miscalculation. Although the flight of some 200,000 certainly gave an impulse to the economies of the Protestant refuges like the Netherlands and England, Scoville's work has shown that the economic effects on France have been greatly exaggerated (**122**). Nevertheless, the measure was effective neither in doing away with the community, since Protestants remained remarkably stalwart in their faith, nor in establishing Louis' religious uniformity. The Revocation greatly alarmed the Protestant powers and facilitated William of Orange's task of constructing a coalition against France. The propaganda of Protestant exiles such as Pierre Jurieu marks a turning point in views of the French monarchy, which was henceforth increasingly identified with tyranny or despotism. The *Sighs of France Enslaved* (1689–90), probably written by Michel Levassor, is an important example of this trend (**15**, Pt 3). Resistance to oppression in France finally led the tenacious Huguenot peasant community in the Cévennes (the Camisards) to rise up in revolt after a particularly brutal episode of fanatical Catholicism in 1702. The revolt drew French troops away from the War of the Spanish Succession until 1707 (**133**).

The persecution of the Jansenists is the second major episode in the attempt to impose religious uniformity on the King's subjects. For Louis, the Jansenists were a sect whose individualism was potentially dangerous, especially as some of its protectors had been leading *Frondeurs**. Several others, such as the members of the Arnauld clan, came from distinguished robe* families at the Paris bar. Their individualism was manifest in the solitary life led by several leading lawyers and aristocrats who had given up worldly pleasures to sojourn at the convent of Port-Royal, dedicating themselves to study and prayer (**171**). Theirs was a personal relationship with God, a relationship that dispensed with hierarchy and intermediaries. But Louis was no theologian, and his prejudices stemmed from the orchestrated hostility towards Jansenism of the Jesuits, who were powerful at court. The *Augustinus* of Cornelius Jansen in 1640 had been a devastating attack on the laxity of the Jesuit doctrine of grace, and Antoine Arnauld's *De la fréquente Communion* (1643) was a treatise that criticised the tolerant morality of the Jesuits (reflecting, as it did, that of the contemporary world), whose policy it was to win souls by a more easy-going, Humanist attitude to social practices.

The condemnation in 1653 and 1655 of the Five Propositions which were alleged to summarise the essence of Jansenism, had been followed by the drawing up of a Formulary to be signed by all clerics. Mazarin's need for internal peace, a well-timed miracle of the Holy Thorn, and Pascal's *Provincial Letters* (1656–57) slowed enforcement of the Formulary until 1661, while Port-Royal found favour with certain elements at court. Then, with royal approval, the war of words hotted up. From 1664, real intimidation, mental cruelty and persecution going as far as internal exile and imprisonment by the church authorities, began in earnest and lasted four years. It was no longer sufficient for Jansenists to sign the Formulary with mental reservations – only complete mental capitulation would do. Four bishops protested and appealed to Rome. Gallican fears of appearing to submit to Rome, if the appeal were to go further, led to the Peace of the Church in 1668.

The period from 1668 to 1679 was the last great age of Jansenism, the 'autumn' of religious Jansenism, as Sainte-Beuve put it in his multi-volume *History of Port-Royal*. The monastery of Port-Royal des Champs was protected by several leading court families, who visited it frequently and made the Jansenist religious, educational and moral ideas ever more popular. The movement had already had a profound influence on the age through its distinguished literary productions, from Pascal to Racine, not forgetting the educational innovations made in the *Petites écoles*. However, persecution was renewed from 1679, after the Peace of Nymegen, with the monastery being forbidden to receive any more novices – a restriction which, in effect, marked the beginning of the end for the first great phase of Jansenism (**169**). Theological quarrels smouldered on, however, and from 1698 broke out again more seriously. A network seems to have existed for the printing and dissemination of tracts in the pamphlet war against the Jesuits.

Analysis

The discovery of the papers of the Jansenist theologian Quesnel, captured in Brussels when he fled the French invasion, persuaded Louis that his fears of the movement as an organised 'republican' conspiracy were well founded.

Louis persuaded the Pope to issue the Bull *Vineam domini*, in 1705, which extended the condemnation of Jansenism; but on Gallican grounds the Assembly of the Clergy and the parlement* only published it with reservations, much to the disappointment of the King. In October 1709, Louis had the remaining twelve nuns at Port-Royal deported to other convents, and in 1711 the buildings were razed to the ground. This solved nothing, because by then Jansenism had developed into a *cause célèbre* that divided the court and involved a great part of the lower clergy. The Bull *Unigenitus* of 1713, again solicited from the reluctant Pope by an increasingly ultramontane Louis, only provoked a worse public debate. Many divines claimed, and they were not far wrong, that the 101 propositions condemned in *Unigenitus* were in fact pure and long-accepted Catholic theology. The outraged Jansenists soon appealed to a council of the church, and won Gallican support for their action (**175**). Louis was to die well before this new phase reached its heights of schismatic controversy.

Some historians, after L. Goldmann's *The Hidden God* (1955), have seen in Jansenism a covert and sublimated movement of political opposition to the 'absolutism' of Louis XIV, on the part of the legal profession. Leaving aside the greatly exaggerated idea such historians have of the enforced subordination of the judicial milieu to the state – hardly credible in the light of new research on the parlements*(**170**) – the rooting of Jansenism in the legal bourgeoisie* can be explained more simply. A high degree of literacy and theological knowledge was necessary to follow the debates, and that was to be found in legal and some courtly circles. It is well, also, to take seriously the idea that Jansenists were motivated primarily by theological considerations, and not to search too hard for oversimplified sociological underpinnings: there was a real preoccupation with personal salvation in a profoundly religious age (**171**). Not until the 1720s did a new and popular Jansenism develop that attracted the common people of Paris (**216**).

The fears of Louis were exaggerated, and it was probably a mistake for him to encourage persecution. It was an error to side entirely with the Jesuits, who were only one faction at court, because this contradicted the more sensible traditional royal policy of holding a balance between factions. The Jesuits acquired too much influence over royal policy in other areas, such as patronage, because the religious issue divided the court in such a way that the favour of the Jesuit group, which included Madame de Maintenon and the King's confessor, became essential for patronage and political advancement. We might also note that, in retrospect, the later victory of the Jansenists over the Jesuits in the eighteenth century (1764) did much to undermine royal authority, which had become tied too closely to the Jesuits during the reign of Louis XIV. Nevertheless, it is not difficult to understand Louis' views when they are placed in their contemporary perspective. He feared schism in the church, he feared resistance, he regarded religious dissent as an affront to the unity of the monarchy. The Jansenist theology seemed to contradict his insistence upon orthodoxy, which was characterised by a desire for unity and order both in the institutions of the state and the minds of his subjects.

The famous quarrel between Bossuet and Fénelon, the two most eminent divines of the period, over the Quietism of Madame Guyon, which divided the court, also involved complex theology. Quietism was a form of Catholic mysticism with a long history. It exalted a spiritual abandon and the mystical contemplation of God, to the point almost of indifference to oneself and to the ecclesiastical hierarchy. Suffice it to say here that Louis followed the advice of his confessor and entourage in condemning the mystical current in Catholicism that Madame Guyon seemed to be reviving. Fénelon, who had supported her, was exiled to his see in Cambrai and fell from favour for a while, until his anti-Jansenism led to his rehabilitation (**29**; **41**, ch. 7). The Quietist movement is a reminder of the diversity of currents in the Catholic church, a diversity which Louis found inimical. Even so, there is litle doubt that Louis was genuinely pious, that he became increasingly so, and that he took his royal duty as defender of the church seriously. Madame de Maintenon supported pious works, particularly her school for young ladies at Saint-Cyr, and encouraged him in his religious observance. Indeed, this was a part of the basis of her power at court. Whenever he could, Louis sought to appoint well-trained bishops who would take care of their flock according to the canons of the Catholic Reformation. In spite of the serious controversies that threatened the tranquillity of the church, scarcely avoidable in such a turbulent century, his reign was an age of Catholic expansion, a period of the Catholic conquest of souls.

6　The Later Decades

The second half of the personal rule had a different atmosphere from the preceding years. The Truce of Ratisbon in 1684 may have marked the apogee of the power of the King, but it was not to last. The revocation of the Edict of Nantes in 1685 signals a turning point, both ideologically, because from then on accusations of tyranny were frequent, and politically, because of the alienation of Protestant Europe from French alliances. The politics of grandeur began to ring hollow. Even so, the regal tone never faltered; grandiose assertions of royal power continued apace; the monarchical order of things became fixed, apparently immutable. Versailles was the centre of government, and it was said you could set your watch by the royal routine. Nevertheless, from 1689 to 1715 there were only five years of peace, and the long years of warfare exacted a heavy price from the monarchy. They were to have a great effect upon the evolution of the state and on its relations with the social classes that formed the basis of the baroque structure. The wars and royal policies were to stimulate an internal critique and virulent foreign propaganda, which undermined the stately façade to the extent that few were sorry to see the end of the reign.

The court and politics

The regimentation or imposition of order on society, as church and state conjoined their efforts, proceeded, if not apace, at least perceptibly. This was the time when the Catholic Reformation made its real impact in France, when the end of 'pagan' ways and the need for order were preached from the pulpit and imposed in the confessional (**176**). The greatest symbol of this monarchical success was the château of Versailles. Although Louis spent a great deal of time at Versailles from 1670 onwards, and the wing designed to house the administration (the *aile des ministres*) was completed in 1663, the château was finally established as the permanent seat of government from 1682. It was more grandiose than it was comfortable. The rooms and corridors were draughty, it was freezing in winter, and unhygienic. No one seemed to appreciate the gardens except the King and the Princess Palatine, to the extent that most courtiers would only visit the park on the occasion of royal promenades or fêtes. Perhaps 10,000 courtiers and their lackeys were crammed into the palace and its environs, and royal life became an object of permanent attention. Soon the need for isolation began to tell on the ageing King; he slept more and more often in the Grand Trianon, built next door to the château, where his family and mistress had apartments. For some of the time the King was on extended stay at Marly, a small château a good carriage-ride away, in the company of chosen courtiers who therefore had good access to him – 'Sire, Marly, Marly . . .', they would beg as he passed by. This did not prevent him from keeping up the practice of work with his ministers, but it did mean that the palace was increasingly more his symbolic than his real residence. His piety increased with his age, entertainments were less frequent and by the turn of the century courtiers were looking to Paris more. His brother's wife, Madame, the Princess Palatine, wrote in 1704:

> No one talks much at court nowadays, and argument has absolutely died out. Most people gamble all the time, and there is nothing that could be called conversation. It is quite out of fashion. People like me and a few others who do not gamble are held in the utmost scorn. . . . The court is not what it used to be, and the only people who gather together are those who are plotting something. Everyone else lives furtively, and there is no gaiety anywhere. (9 March 1704)

The atmosphere was changing in the arts too. There was a move away from the style and conviction of the early years. The doctrinaire insistence on the superiority of the King to antique heroes, combined with the loss of creative conviction in a style so overworked, was to lead to a transformation and a decline in the quality of royal propaganda. To some extent this was inevitable, for the writers of the first two decades of the personal rule had sung the praises of the King in every way they could imagine. As we have seen, a discourse developed in which elaborate analogies and metaphors were drawn between classical gods and heroes – Apollo, Hercules, Jupiter, Mars, for example – and Louis. Naturally enough these metaphors became stale and, in the hands of lesser writers, lost their power to convince. This was simply because, if the King had surpassed the ancients, metaphors were no longer forceful enough, and direct discussion of the King's virtues still carried with it a sense of sacrilege. So mythology tended to become an ornament, and there was a move from the powerful language of metaphor to the pleasing suggestion of allegory (**196**). The best example of this is in the decoration of the Hall of Mirrors by Lebrun, which portrayed the King's real exploits in allegorical form (**209**). Louis himself was changing, and his taste in the monumental declined. From the 1690s his art collection was his great interest, rather than architecture, the pageant or the theatre. The final consequence was a move away from inventive allegories towards a more rigid classicism that had lost all power to convince.

In 1683 the Queen died, and it was probably in the following year that the King's secret marriage to Madame de Maintenon took place. Although she had nominally been only the governess of the royal bastards, she had displaced Madame de Montespan in the King's affections some years earlier. Her *dévôt** attitudes, evident from the mid-1680s, became an important element in court politics. From 1686 she became *dévôte* and began to undertake the conversion of Louis to greater piety (**55**). She and the King's confessor, Père Le Tellier, even though they were rivals, succeeded in channelling patronage towards the Jesuit clique to the extent that advancement in any sphere depended partly on this issue. The increasingly *dévôt* atmosphere, already noted in the chapter on religion, made itself felt in many areas of courtly life and policy. The changes in the royal attitude towards the Pope made possible the reconciliation of 1693; from then on the King was decidedly anti-Gallican because he was so anti-Jansenist. Naturally, the court split into two factions, Jansenist and Jesuit. Madame de Maintenon supported the Colbert family, which had strong ties to the *dévôt* faction, thus enabling them to regain during the 1690s the prominence they had lost in the 1680s, when the Le Telliers dominated.

The divine-right monarchy had dynastic preoccupations, not only in foreign policy but also at home. The throne was passed on through the male line and this had to be assured. The Bourbon clan was extensive when one considers the collateral lines of Orléans, Condé and Conti, who were princes of the blood. If they seemed unlikely to resort to force, these families still harboured pretensions to political power. Louis had not only to keep them out of the council but also ensure a smooth succession. The direct line seemed secure because the Grand Dauphin*, addressed as Monseigneur, who was born in 1661, had three male children. The eldest, the Duc de Bourgogne, was born in 1682; the second, the Duc d'Anjou, born in 1683, was chosen as the King of Spain in 1701 and renounced his rights to the French succession; the third, the Duc de Berri, was born in 1686 but died in 1714. The marriage of the Duc de Bourgogne to Marie-Adelaide of Savoy produced three sons, all named Louis, in 1704, 1707 and 1710, but the first died in infancy. As if to show how precarious a seemingly strong line could be, the Grand Dauphin died of smallpox in 1711, and with the help of incompetent doctors, measles carried off in turn the Duc de Bourgogne, his wife and the second son. The third son, Louis, survived only because his governesses refused to allow him to be treated. (See the family tree on p. 157.) It must be said that the Grand Dauphin had been much disliked, and had displayed little interest in politics and even less competence. As for the Duc de Bourgogne, he had been educated in such a theoretical way that his experience of the world was pitifully inadequate, and even if his intentions were of the best his will was weak. He was a man of such extreme piety and conscience that the prospect of reigning had terrified him; he seemed almost pleased to escape his fate by dying. The throne would now pass to the new and sickly infant, Louis, but in the short term a regency was inevitable.

Before the run of tragic deaths, Louis had pursued a policy of allying his illegitimate children with the houses of the Princes of the Blood, whom he had resolutely kept distanced from affairs of state. The Duc du Maine (1670–1736) was married to a Bourbon-Condé; the Comte de Toulouse (1678–1737) married into a much-favoured non-princely family, the Noailles; Louis' natural daughters from La Vallière and Montespan married a Conti, a Condé and an Orléans. The latter was destined to become Regent in 1715. The King was sorely troubled at the prospect of a Regency under the Duc d'Orléans, whose libertine sentiment and escapades were notorious. Louis tried a solution that went right against the French legal tradition by legitimising his bastards Maine and Toulouse in 1714. This not only conferred succession rights on them after the Princes of the Blood, but also gave them entry to the councils which governed France. Louis had hoped by these means to provide a counterweight to the Regent, but, predictably enough, Philippe, Duc d'Orléans had the Paris parlement* set aside all the King's attempts in his will to influence matters after his death.

During the later decades of the reign, Louis worked ever harder at being his own first minister, devoting more time to business and less to entertainments. He still followed his policy of balancing the factions, but encouraged the Phélypeaux clan's rise to prominence at the end of the 1680s. Louis Phélypeaux, Comte de Pontchartrain, was made controller-general, and given the departments of the marine and the *maison du roi* (the King's household). This was the same powerful concentration of offices that Colbert himself had held. In 1699, when the old Chancellor Boucherat died (**80**), the much younger Pontchartrain (he was fifty-six) took his place and put new vigour into the office. His son became secretary for the marine with responsibility also for the King's household, and the La Vrillière branch carried on as secretaries of state (**78**).

After the death of Louvois in 1691, the Le Tellier clan lost its pre-eminence as the King had no confidence in the minister's son, who was a drunkard. Power during the last two decades was therefore shared between the Colbert and the Phélypeaux clans. Colbert de Torcy died in 1696 and was succeeded as secretary of state and minister for foreign affairs by his well-trained son, the Marquis de Torcy. The King had him marry Pomponne's daughter, and this reluctant match drew the Pomponne family into the Colbert network (**145**, ch. 12). The Duc de Beauvillier, now in charge of the education of the Duc de Bourgogne, was a nephew of Colbert, as was the influential Duc de Chevreuse. From 1707 the controller-generalship was held by Desmaretz, who was Torcy's cousin and thus another nephew of Colbert. Of course, these families had powerful protectors amongst the well-established aristocratic houses, and it may well be true to say that faction was crucial in maintaining their position. Right up until the end of the reign the central government was therefore characterised by the dominance of powerful clans sustained in court politics by faction and intrigue. It was a system that Louis XIV, who insisted on having the last word, encouraged.

The study of the methods and rivalries of the ministers reveals a system of personal relations that was a far cry from the so-called 'administrative monarchy'. There was of course a large measure of bureaucratic routine in these jobs, but at their highest levels they reflected the continuation of patrimonialism. Charles Frostin has revealed, in his studies of Pontchartrain, that the accumulation of tasks reflected the power of the individual, as well as of the clan, perhaps more than that of the bureaucratic office. He notes the

very personalised character of political office, the fiction of the unity of the central government, the limits of the power of the controller generalship of finances, and above all the importance of the combination of the marine with the king's household. (**79**, p. 201)

Colbert had not transformed the finances into a chief ministry, as is proved by the relative obscurity of his successors in the 1680s. Furthermore, the ministers were constantly trying to expand their power at one another's expense. Jerôme de Pontchartrain from 1699 to 1715 was constantly encroaching on the duties of the secretary for foreign affairs and the controller-general (**79**). His father, Pontchartrain, had been the patron of a financial clan, just as Colbert had been before him, which had helped him to finance the War of the League of Augsburg. As Chancellor, Pontchartrain behaved not as a bureaucrat but as the grand patron or protector of the magistrates. His relations with the first presidents of the parlements* were personalised and were all the more effective for being so.

> In a strong position by virtue of his own past as a magistrate and his close kinship ties with distinguished *parlementaire* families, strengthened too by the robe solidarities which led the judicial officers to see in him one of their own kind, in his task of making himself obeyed, Louis de Pontchartrain benefited from the real advantages of confidence and above all competence. (**77**, p. 32)

The Chancellor was firm, but diplomatic and conciliatory in his dealings.

These conclusions are reinforced by recent studies of the clerks in the bureaux of the ministers of war and foreign affairs. Rule and Baxter both conclude that even at the end of the reign family, fidelity and clientage were more important than bureaucratic structures. The two could coexist, of course; Rule concludes that 'The patron/client relationship is still intact in 1715; indeed, in the foreign office, it may be stronger than it was in 1680. However, the bureaucratic machinery has, it would appear, become somewhat better articulated' (**73**, p. 77). According to Baxter, summarising his work on the war department, while 'much further work needs to be done to pinpoint the decline of the clientage system and the emergence of a new, more impersonal civil service, . . . evidence in the war department suggests that it was much later, in the eighteenth century, than Antoine proposes' (**74**, p. 84). Taken together, these studies provide grounds for rejecting the thesis that Louis' reign saw the emergence of an administrative monarchy.

Analysis

It was hard to enact any coherent programme of reform in wartime. Chamillart was unable to raise enough money for the campaigns and was succeeded by Desmaretz as controller-general in September 1707, but he continued as war minister. At this stage in the war France was on the verge of complete disaster and lacked direction in government. Fénelon wrote to the Duc de Chevreuse on 3 December 1708:

> Monsieur de Chamillart told me, when he passed by here, that everything was in desperate straits for carrying on the war. But Monsieur de Chamillart, who was strongly arguing our power-lessness to continue the war, said, on the one hand, that we couldn't sue for peace with dishonourable terms. For my part, I was tempted to say to him: either make war better, or don't make it at all; if you go on doing it this way, the peace terms will be even more shameful in a year than they are today; you can only lose by waiting.... They lack everything, both in the strong-holds in case of siege, and in the armies, because of the lack of money.... There is no single person in control of affairs, nor anyone who dares take anything upon himself. Direction, given in the days of M. de Louvois, is no more; money and the force of command are lacking; there is no one who is up to reestab-lishing these two essential points.... We are ruining and risking France for Spain. (**71**, p. 256)

In the event, Louis saved France from his enemies by exacting further sacrifices from his people, which gave him just enough time to profit from the break-up of the Grand Alliance. Of chief concern here is the way in which the government of the state evolved under these pressures. On the one hand, they stimulated a critique of the system and prompted reform projects for the system of public finance and taxation, as well as a more consultative style of government (**39**). On the other hand, the pressures were so great that the whole system degenerated. We have seen before that foreign war placed enormous strain on the inefficient fiscal struc-tures. The system of naval recruitment had never functioned properly, as resistance and the urgent necessities of war under-mined it from the start (**178**). Provinces far from the battlefields were reluctant to contribute to the cost of a war that did not directly concern them. The demands were too great, local resis-tance was too effective and the peasants were too poor for taxes to be fully collected. It is hard to see how Louis could ever have been credited with setting up a system of centralised government when the keynotes of the later decades are so obviously expediency and compromise. This point is clearly revealed by the reconsideration of the royal intendants*.

The intendants in perspective

Understandably, much of the interpretation of the reign of Louis XIV has turned upon a certain view of the efficiency and achievements of the intendants*. For those historians who equate orders and statements with achievements under the *ancien régime**, the intendants may be said to have provided France with an efficient, centralised bureaucracy. They personify the triumph of the commissioner over the venal official*, and *a fortiori* the triumph of the modern state over the particularism of local interests (**19, 94, 86**). This is a tenacious view first expressed at length by Lemontey, and given substance if not weight by historians under the Third Republic in France, whose studies often read between the lines like wishful thinking for the kind of administrative order and centralisation that politicians were then imposing on French society. Yet, recent research has undermined their belief in a coherent policy of centralisation under Louis XIV, and those early historians who doubted the actual triumph of the administration over the localities should now be paid closer attention (**95, 94, 97**). Indeed, we should question the existence of any overall scheme or intention on the part of the central government except the idea of maximising the tax receipts. Thus, the attempt to subject the municipalities to closer control by the intendants was not an attempt at centralisation *per se*, it was simply a device to reduce debts and ensure that towns were in a position to pay taxes and lend more to the crown later. Although the intendants were the eyes and ears of the ministers in the provinces, they were warned not to usurp the powers of local bodies [**doc. 22**]. Contrary to opinion, their commissions did not give them all-embracing authority. There are isolated examples of intervention in almost every area of the administration, but sustained intervention was rare, and it was most often achieved by means of a report to the council of state. Judging from the few regional studies that are available, it seems that each intendant was expected to adapt himself to the situation in his *généralité**, which varied greatly. The task of an intendant in Provence, where he managed the representative Assembly of Communities in conjunction with other prominent figures, like the Archbishop of Aix and the lieutenant-general of the province (**40**), was different from that in Alsace, where he was expected to do his utmost to attach the province to France (**90**; **44**, ch. 9). In Orléans he had much greater direct power, but was almost entirely concerned with taxation and order (**93**); in Languedoc he helped the governor to manage the provincial Estates, which really administered the province with the parlement*, and tried to enforce the Edict of Fontainebleau (**96**). In wartime, in all the frontier provinces especially, much time would be devoted to the problem of moving soldiers and ensuring supplies.

Studies of the intendants* as a corps of officials (they were mostly masters of requests*), and detailed work on the provinces, reveal them to have been concerned with their own advancement, beset by problems stemming from local resistance, starved of resources and dependent on the power of patronage as well as on bureaucratic methods (**37**, **32**, **88**). From the great nineteenth-century collections of published documents (**1**, **2**, **3**), the overwhelming impression is of men instructed to help with the war effort by maximising taxes, minimising public protest and disorder, and organising recruitment, billeting and supplies for the army. This was a continuation of their function under Richelieu and Mazarin (**86**). Although their role was to evolve during the eighteenth century, it seems that under Louis XIV they continued to be instruments of war, rather than administrators in the modern sense (**88**). A balanced appreciation of their work would emphasise their efforts and short-term achievements, but be more careful not to exaggerate their long-term effect in this period. Some, like Basville in Languedoc and Colbert de Croissy in Alsace, who both spent many years in their province, had a real effect because they exerted constant and unremitting pressure on the locality. Others, like intendant Foucault in Grenoble and then Montauban, would be highly loyal and competent but were moved on to new tasks before they could complete even as important a work as the elimination of municipal debts. Still others were too ready to compromise with local vested interests and were too anxious to present a rosy picture so that they could return to Paris or the Ile de France. All were obliged to use local officials as their sub-delegates, but these were men who naturally knew and protected local interests.

Although Colbert often complained about the intendants'* choice of sub-delegates to help them, and repeatedly condemned their use, he at the same time heaped work on the intendants. In the later years of the reign, however, his successor Chamillart, once an intendant, fully recognised the need for such helpers. They were almost always men who were already officers of justice or finance, or mayors. 'At the end of the seventeenth century', Ricommard believes, 'the sub-delegates had become as it were the intendants' "men", in the feudal sense of the term' (**75**, p. 146). Since they were unpaid, and were rewarded by gratifications obtained for them, the intendants tended to treat them carefully. When about 600 offices of sub-delegate were created for sale in 1704, most intendants tried to get a reduction on the price for their helpers. Later still, when Desmaretz tried to squeeze more money out of them, the intendants intervened tacitly in their favour, with the result that the attempt was a total failure. But in the long run, venality of office* had the effect of identifying the office with a fixed circumscription, while intendancies too came to be definitively attached to a town and a *généralité**. The administrative map of France was thus gradually becoming more clearly defined, with permanent intendancies broken down into lesser areas under sub-delegates in the eighteenth century. However, the problem was that 'there are numerous examples of sub-delegates who, from the second half of the seventeenth century, firmly took the part of local interests against the intendant or even the controller-general' (**75**, p. 147). And the intendants usually defended them against the controller-general. This situation is typical of the ambiguities in the practice of government during the *ancien régime**.

Financing the wars

The factor which most undermined the reforms of the early decades and warped the development of the monarchy was war finance (**61**). In 1687 the royal military budget was around 54 million *livres**. It jumped to 103 million just two years later in 1689, rose to 138 million in 1692, and remained at well over 100 million a year till 1698. The same thing happened during the War of the Spanish Succession. From 55 million *livres* in 1700, war expenditure reached 104 million in 1701 and continued to rise until 1713 (see Appendix 2 and 3, III, pp. 615–22). Where was all the money to come from? Recent attempts to answer this question lead us to a new understanding of the social basis of the regime.

As we have seen, the *taille** weighed heavily on the peasantry, whose poverty imposed limits on the level of direct taxation. Those in society who had the money largely escaped taxation by virtue of their privileges* and exemptions. Thus, the huge sums of ready cash required for military ventures were in fact largely in the hands of the rich. The problem for the monarchy was how to lay hands on this money, especially as its problem of revenue was compounded by a chronic shortage of coin [**doc. 19**]. The obvious but socially and politically impossible solution was to tax the rich by overruling their exemptions. This was in fact tried twice, with the *capitation** of 1695 and the *dixième** of 1710. Neither of these new taxes was very successful, and although radical in conception, in practice neither constituted a fundamental reform of the system (**32**). The church bought itself off with an increased *don gratuit* (free gift), and the privileged classes so strongly defended their exemptions that after the first couple of years the taxes were reduced to more or less an addition to the *taille*. Nor did the ministry expect much more than this – being perhaps rather more realistic about social and political possibilities than later ministries. It is worth remembering that it was an attempt to do away with fiscal privilege that led in 1787 to the collapse of the *ancien régime**.

The lack of fundamental reform of the financial system explains the continuing importance of the iniquitous but usual 'extraordinary affairs' (**138, 140**). These were a wide range of governmental expedients which ranged from the raising of loans and life annuities on alienated capital, known as *rentes**, to forced loans, the sale of offices, titles and *privilèges**, and the institution of a host of 'taxes' levied on new and sometimes far-fetched projects. The word 'taxes' must be used loosely, because in most cases the sums were raised by selling offices, *rentes* or privileges to the moderately wealthy. The ministry often marketed a combination of office and wider privileges to make 'the goods' (as Pontchartrain cynically called the offices) more saleable (**136**, p. 16). He joked to the King that 'Every time Your Majesty creates an office, God creates a fool to buy it'. Loans were vitally important. One of the most ruinous devices was the *tontine*, whereby a creditor advanced capital and received a rate of interest worked out by dividing the lenders into age-groups with a fixed rate for the group; but as the lenders died off increased sums would be paid to the survivors until the last one in the group died. This was ruinous for the monarchy because it ended up paying out much more than the advance was worth, yet *tontines* were used increasingly from 1689.

This system of *affaires extraordinaires* was dependent upon the participation of financiers – known as *partisans** or *traitants** – who acted as providers of funds which they would advance to the treasury in return for a contract to recover the principal from those taxed or buying the offices and so on [**docs 31, 32**]. (It was usually a question of some new tax or new batch of offices.) The controller-general would surround himself with *donneurs d'avis* who would think up projects, propose them and take a substantial 'tip' or *pot de vin*, while the financier might take a cut as high as 25 per cent of the expected revenue. There were vast sums to be made, and courtly women often played the role of go-between, as did established financiers like Poisson de Bourvalais (**136**). This man was the leading financier of the later period. He owed his rise to the protection of Pontchartrain, who relied on him and ensured his immunity from prosecution on several occasions. He specialised in the traffic of offices and was involved in well over 100 *traités* (contracts) out of 600 from 1688 to 1715. One particularly unsavoury episode was the La Noue affair: in 1699, the unfortunate and equally corrupt La Noue was on the verge of bankruptcy; he transferred many of his assets to his friend Bourvalais, with the aim of recovering them later, after his bankruptcy; but Chamillart, the controller-general, and Desmaretz, La Noue's former protector, as well as Bourvalais decided that it was more profitable to sacrifice La Noue than to protect him; in 1703, therefore, La Noue was condemned to nine years in the galleys. Bourvalais kept much of the fortune that La Noue had so unwisely signed away, and Desmaretz, later as controller-general, had the pleasure of refusing the unfortunate financier his pleas for liberty (**136**, ch. 3). The world of financiers that was so viciously lampooned in contemporary pamphlets and plays was every bit as corrupt and nasty as they said; but it was not half as bourgeois* – it was mostly aristocratic! Naturally, the successful men of money rose in society, made fine marriages with the aristocracy and built mansions on large estates ... like Colbert and Fouquet (**140**, chs 5 and 6)!

Paradoxically, much of the money that was obtained by the extraordinary affairs actually came from the royal revenues by way of the receivers-general for the provinces or for the army (**57**). As private managers of money, responsible for centralising the taxes, and independent because they owned their offices, these men could postpone payment to the crown and act as bankers with the funds which they held, often getting away with massive fraud. Their position in society gave them the air of security which made the provincial bourgeoisie*, nobility and rich church institutions willing to lend to them, or invest in their projects. But an enormous amount of cash came directly from the court aristocracy who used the lesser financiers as middlemen in order to mask their own involvement. Most financiers held royal offices themselves and many were in the employ of the richest aristocratic houses, as financial advisers (**140**, chs 4 and 5).

The intendants* helped the financiers to find likely buyers for offices and were expected to protect the *traitants** in their region from legal pursuit or popular hatred on account of their rapacity. This task cast the intendants in the role of oppressors, and accounts in part for such unfavourable assessments as that of Saint-Simon [**doc. 20**]. But since the intendants had protected, and continued to protect, the rural communities from local potentates who tried to transfer the burden of taxes on to them, they could easily end up with divided loyalties, as much inclined to defend their province as to help squeeze more money out of it.

The *taille** was the basic and constant royal tax that enabled loans to be raised. But, as the ever-increasing number of venal offices* carried privileges exempting the owners from paying the *taille* or lodging troops, the tax burden fell more heavily on the poor. The intendant* of Metz wrote in 1695:

> In order to gain exemption from the constant obligations of giving lodging to soldiers, almost all the burgers who have anything at all have acquired offices as recorders of seizures, sworn experts, surveyors, baptismal clerks and so on, for the list is too long. Other inhabitants are now trying to gain immunity by becoming clerks to the *traitants**, for the distribution of letters, the receipt of debts, the distribution of stamped paper, the supply of tobacco and similar jobs. The tax farmers and *traitants* have orders in council which exempt all their clerks. (**136**)

Thus it was that the King borrowed from the rich and transferred the tax burden 'on to the rest of the people, as if it was the country of an enemy' (Boisguilbert, **16**, pp. 61–2). Since the community was taxed as a community, anyone gaining exemption simply passed on the tax to someone else. The intendant* of Alençon wrote in 1702: 'The problem is particularly severe in the towns, where the richest bourgeois can exempt themselves for 200 *livres**, or even less, from billeting, the collection of the *taille** and any increase in it.' The recrudescence of local disturbances and the profound misery of the populace that was so evident in 1694 and 1709, was the result of this inequitable and makeshift financial system [**doc. 18**]. A second result was the extraordinary proliferation of minor offices which give the misleading impression of the development of an administrative monarchy (**57**, ch. 3). The third result was that the monarchy was very much in the hands of those who provided the money – namely, the wealthy aristocrats of church and court, who channelled their surplus wealth through the financiers into state finances. As Dessert rightly points out, the monarchy could not reform its financial system without attacking the court aristocracy, whose protection of the financiers made even *chambres de justice** only a partial solution (**140**, chs 10 and 11). Such attacks could not succeed because they undermined the credit so desperately needed by the crown in its hour of need.

There developed during the seventeenth century, and especially in the reign of Louis XIV, a kind of equilibrium or tacit bargain between elite and state – in so far as they were separate – in which the King provided prestige and order, and a guarantee of social stability, in return for a share in the spoils of the system. In Languedoc, 'The notables got more money back from the king, and they had greater control over what he spent in the province' (**37**, p. 269). Everywhere, the *parlementaires* and local notables were allowed to retain their privileges*, frequently confirmed in royal letters, as long as they cooperated with the fiscal demands. It is a testimony to the inherent strength of France and to this careful management of the elite by the crown, that burdens at least as heavy as those that provoked the *Frondes** were borne without a complete collapse of the system. It was no longer in the interests of the local elites to allow such disturbances.

Criticism of the royal policies

The fiscal demands of the royal government dramatically increased as the wars dragged on. Even with recourse to all the old expedients of the 1650s – expedients that Colbert himself had fallen back on – the controllers-general of the last two decades of the reign were at their wits' end to pay for the campaigns. Inevitably, criticisms of the monarchy and its style became more frequent. Studies of royalist propaganda in literature and the other arts have shown the 1680s to have been a watershed. This was partly for political reasons: the Revocation of the Edict of Nantes led to an exodus of bitter Huguenots whose writings tended to portray Louis as a religious tyrant (**202**, **185**, **187**). Inside

France there were growing reservations about the increasing power of the monarchy. The 1690s saw the elaboration of a careful critique of Louis' system by the aristocratic circle of thinkers and men of action associated with the education of the Duc de Bourgogne, who was likely to become king in due course. Fénelon (**13**), Boulainvilliers (**190**), Boisguilbert, the Abbé de Saint-Pierre (**189**) and the Duc de Saint-Simon were the theorists; the Ducs de Chaulnes, Chevreuse and Noailles were provincial governors and trusted military commanders quite close to the King, while Vauban was both a theorist and a man of action (**32, 187, 188**).

The views of the 'Circle of the Duke of Burgundy' have often been misread and characterised as the outpourings of a feudal aristocracy deprived of power (e.g., **58**). Nothing could be further from the truth. These men were well placed to witness and analyse the ills of wartime France. The famous reports of the intendants* on the *généralités**, now a major source for historians, were originally drawn up for the education of the Duc de Bourgogne. The slipshod way many of them were prepared justifies the criticism of the intendants by Boulainvilliers in his *Etat de la France* (London, 1736). There are too many different approaches and strands to the thought of the Circle to discuss in detail. Suffice it to say that their analysis was acute and their suggestions far from unrealistic. They did indeed advocate a return to aristocratic rule, but mainly because they saw the power and independence of the nobility as a defence against tyranny. They were particularly troubled by the extension of monarchical power into the provinces without proper knowledge of local interests or conditions. Their solution was to set up consultative institutions in all the provinces, dominated by the nobility, which they regarded as a more responsible group than it probably was. However, their taxation projects, such as the *capitation** and *dixième**, envisaged an end to noble exemptions, and their nobility was to be one whose rank was justified by service, and not simply by its feudal origins (**13, 191**). Some of their ideas were very anachronistic, some were drawn from the contemporary situation and some had a large influence in the eighteenth century on political thought. Such writers, even if they were mostly unable to publish until after the death of Louis, bear witness to the 'crisis of consciousness' at the beginning of the eighteenth century, and to the continued potential for innovative thought in the France of Louis XIV (**183**).

The economy

The conventional view has long been that the economy was in stagnation and recession during the reign of Louis XIV, and that this depression was aggravated by government policy. War taxation, an excess of regulations, restraints on trade and the loss of skilled labour provoked by the flight of Protestants, combined to depress the market for manufactures while preventing innovation (**28**, Bk.13; **27**). However, this traditional picture has been challenged by some historians. Regional studies have shown that there was no French economy as a whole, that it was more a question of regional economies. Provence, for example, apparently began to revive from the 1680s, well before France as a whole. The agricultural economy was indeed in a poor state, with the receipts of the clerical tenth going down by 15–30 per cent during the reign. But the terrible subsistence crises of 1693–94 and 1709 had no lasting effects and may have kept wages high. Nor were these crises of equal gravity in the different regions. Brittany, Picardy and Maine suffered little, while in Anjou the impact was severe although few died; the south was relatively spared. The good harvests of 1710 led to a speedy recovery. Nevertheless, everywhere rural indebtedness by the peasants, provoked by high taxation and agricultural stagnation or decline, led to what Le Roi Ladurie has called the 'triumph of *rente**', meaning the social and economic rise of those with money to invest (**111**). This period witnessed the expropriation of the peasantry as its property was bought up by the urban elite and the rural nobility. Land transfer took place and the profits were siphoned off to the towns (**113**).

A different picture is emerging about trade and manufactures. The traditional picture of depression as evidenced by the movement of prices and a decline in imports of precious metals has been called into question. It is important to draw a distinction between the rural interior of France, in all its regional diversity, and the maritime ports with their hinterland. The latter appear to have remained relatively independent of the agricultural depression. There was perhaps a decline in some ports as the result of government policy against trading with the enemy – for example, the commerce of Saint Malo was hit by the maritime wars and the English market for cloth was definitively lost (**8**). On the other hand, many ports thrived as a result of the profitable privateering war against the Maritime Powers. The value of prizes totalled about 220 million *livres** from 1689 to 1713. Trade with Spain, the

Antilles and the Levant continued and even grew. Carrière has shown in his study of Marseille that, contrary to the view in previous works, the port was not in decline, and that a revival began in the 1690s (121). This happened well after Colbert, who figures little in the new economic history.

Rather than attribute prosperity or decline to the activity of great men, economic historians now put the accent on long-term structural factors. The problems were due mainly to such factors as the economic depression and the traditional flight of merchant capital into land and privilege*, although the government did compound these difficulties. The most important industry was the manufacture of cloth, employing about 1 million people. It suffered from a profound depression from the 1650s to the early 1690s. Then there was a sharp revival. In an important recent study, Markovitch has shown that the total output of cloth in the main centres of production remained steady or increased in the 1690s and 1700s until 1708. The production of woollens rose from 865,000 pieces in 1700 to 1,121,000 pieces in 1715. The demand for the armies in wartime combined with a bigger Spanish and American market to push production up to the levels attained early in the century, in Amiens for example (44, ch. 11). Thus, care must be taken to avoid blaming the government for a decline that cannot be clearly demonstrated. While it is true that some 200,000 Huguenots fled from France, their loss was probably more than compensated for by the immigration of Catholics from England and Ireland. The international financial network and trading links established by the Huguenot exiles actually benefited France in the long run (44, ch. 13). So too with the economic factors: war interfered with trade in some quarters but stimulated other sectors. In his survey of the economy during this period, Schaeper concludes that 'The old idea that royal policies were mostly responsible must be rejected once and for all' (121, p. 55).

The monarchy and reform

A similar picture emerges with regard to the central administration. We have seen that although the team of ministers of the post-Louvois period may seem to have lacked the reforming zeal of their predecessors, they were nevertheless extremely able men. As Hatton and Rule have rightly pointed out, in some respects we are justified in detecting a second period of reform (26, 39). The new taxes, the *capitation** and the *dixième** *royal*, are evidence of a willingness to rethink, if also of a lack of power to execute. The Council of Commerce from 1700 bears witness to a recognition of the problems of overregulation of trade and industry and the need for greater consultation (**120**). In some areas there was more bureaucracy, with a slow transition in the department of foreign affairs, and greater regularity in the organisation of the bureaux (**146**, ch. 11; **154**, **73**, **74**). There was a project for training ambassadors in diplomacy organised by François de Callières, who wrote *On the Manner of Negotiating with Princes* (1716). But it has to be emphasised once again that these developments do not amount to a transformation of the state into an administrative monarchy. Under Louis XIV, it still retained many of the characteristics of the baroque state whose long history had so profoundly modelled it.

On 1 September 1715, a few days before his seventy-seventh birthday, the King died. His personal rule had lasted over forty-four years, and towards the end, France and his courtiers had wearied of his rule. It had become immensely oppressive during the war. The fiscal system had been once again stretched to breaking point, yet the monarchy was certainly in debt in 1715 by as much as 1,200 million *livres**, and the figure may well have been 2,000 million *livres* (**135**). Louis was powerless to secure the monarchy against the new spirit that prefigured the Enlightenment. Opposition had been stimulated by the excesses, and censorship did not prevent the circulation of radical and innovative books, such as Bayle's *Dictionnaire*. The myth of all-powerful monarchy that Louis had tried so hard to propagate was in decline and the old regime had become dangerously rigid. The removal of the court to Paris in late 1715 symbolises the changed situation; the *Persian Letters* of Montesquieu were a biting satire on the last decades.

Part Three: Assessment

Assessments of Louis XIV's long reign have varied from praise to condemnation. Goubert launched the first serious modern assault on the King's memory in 1966, but most of his French successors have been more susceptible to the image (**33**). The best biography is still by an American, although it is very much focused on the person of the King to the neglect of France (**47**). In France, biography and institutional history seem to go hand in hand, and most books have taken the image and the regulations of the early decades of the personal rule as the basis of their judgement. In some of the works of the 1930s there is an appeal to sentimentalism as the aged King is portrayed heroically battling on to the end. The monarchy's programme of order has been analysed as if it were a part of the state-building of the Third Republic; some studies have been reminiscent of, and written in, the spirit of Vichy France. The hagiographic tradition masquerading as history seems destined to continue as long as unscholarly studies are republished. 'Whig history', in which new research is inserted into an old framework of explanation, even when it has been undermined, has been given a new lease of life by Bluche (1989), whose volume on Louis places itself firmly in the nationalist tradition (**49**). Before accepting French nationalism as a valid perspective, we should perhaps remember how Louis was seen in the Dutch Republic:

> In spite of the excellent beginnings by the king, his limitless ambition, his boundless love of *gloire*** led him to develop serious faults and even vices. Almost all the Dutch profoundly hated him. They reproached him with his perfidy, his duplicity, his despotism, his vanity, his presumption, his cruelty, his egoism, his hypocrisy, his ruses, his habit of sowing discord everywhere, of corrupting foreign princes and ministers, his dishonest ways of procuring money. At first, Louis was feared, but little by little he ceased to be a danger to the Dutch, at which point the pamphleteers showered him with invective and accusations. (**185**)

[handwritten margin note: Truer more on Louis than on these important other elements.]

Almost all historians agree that there was a decline in the system from the mid-1680s, but studies have focused on the first two decades of the personal rule, to the comparative neglect of the later decades. Detailed modern works are lacking on the economy, the governors, court and faction, on the bishops and *curés* as agents of the state, and on most of the intendants*. These last need to be looked at not in the light of the rise of the modern state, which distorts the contemporary reality, but from the perspective of war administration and the emerging compromise between the crown and the elites. This book has tried to avoid too narrow a focus and has aimed at an overall judgement. However, given this penury of works on the later part of the reign, it would be premature to propose too firm an evaluation of the reign. What follows here is an individual scholar's attempt to draw together into a coherent whole the various strands of a new interpretation.

The people of France, already suffering in a long cyclical depression of trade and agriculture, were indeed sacrificed to the *gloire** of their ruler. The ambitious and injudicious foreign policy of the 1660s and 1670s largely created the difficulties of the later period. That this was foreseeable is proved by a letter from Courtin to Louvois in 1673 [**doc. 34**]. However, we must not go too far down this road, because different, equally serious wars might easily have occurred if policy had been different. The Habsburg Empire was a threat, and the revival of the Habsburg fortunes during the rule of the ambitious and capable Emperor Leopold would no doubt have led to serious conflicts requiring a similar fiscal effort. To a large extent, the royal perspective on this was that the pursuit of *gloire* was entirely legitimate, and that the wars were necessary for the defence of the French kingdom. Research has shown that the first three major wars were caused by the pursuit of glory, but that the War of the Spanish Succession was not desired by the King.

Was Louis an 'absolute monarch', and if so, what does this mean? In the first place, it has to be emphasised that the concept of 'absolute' monarchy coexisted with the notion of areas in which the will of the monarch could not rightfully be exercised. Thus the scope for the legitimate exercise of royal power was still very narrow compared to the sphere of state activity today. Corporate society largely governed itself, and the church was responsible for education. The King was expected to exercise his sovereignty in foreign policy, in the defence of religion, and by the keeping of order in the commonwealth through the provision of justice. He was regarded as an arbiter, keeping a balance in society (**44**). What especially complicates matters is the very long tradition of the royal prerogative, by virtue of which the King could intervene beyond the normal limits of his power in the interests of the common-wealth (or state, as royal jurists were now arguing). In the seventeenth century the King and his advisers were trying to make prerogatives into rights and were devising theoretical arguments to back themselves up (**43**, ch. 8). Struggles in the provinces, for example, often ended in some sort of compromise based on formal recognition of the rights of the monarchy but an actual continuation of the power of local elites. Thus it was that absolute sovereignty meant a great deal less than absolute power.

The argument about the nature of Louis XIV's rule has given rise to a theory of a supposed transition to an 'administrative monarchy' (**44**, ch. 3). It is certainly true that the bureaucracy of the monarchy had changed in some ways since the early seventeenth century, and that administrative structures had been expanded and regularised. The secretaries of state developed small but more regularly organised bureaux: this was particularly true of the foreign affairs department during the last decades of the reign. The intendants* had become a permanent fixture in the provinces, along with their sub-delegates. It is important to remember, however, that these administrative structures and methods were in their infancy, and that there is a difference between origins and basic characteristics (**20**, ch. 3). It was said of Colbert's office that only the reports written by his own hand were well conceived. The new methods and cadres were inserted for *ad hoc* reasons into pre-existing social and political structures that were still largely incompatible with them. They in fact functioned in ways that have usually been described as more modern than they really were.

Institutional historians all too often make the mistake of overvaluing their evidence, by assuming that the text of an administrative document accurately reveals political or social practice. To some extent it may do, but it is important to note that in the early modern era many such documents were declarations of intent, or attempts by jurists to fix a reality that in practice was highly fluid. It is a truism, confirmed by modern regimes today, that channels of power do not necessarily follow the bureaucratic outlines. Furthermore, bureaucracy can conceal the fact that the real decisions have been made in a very different way – as, for example, when an administrative order confirms a decision solicited by patronage.

There is ample and accumulating evidence that patronage, clientage, a whole sophisticated system of favours and gratifications, representation and symbolism, all played an important role in 'governing' Louis XIV's France. The belief in the triumph of an 'administrative monarchy' does not square with what we know of the situation in the eighteenth century. Some historians would now argue that the principal characteristics of the baroque monarchy remained, if not unchanged, at least dominant under Louis XV. After Louis XIV, as before, inefficiencies, corruption (especially in tax assessments), patronage and clientage all continued to be important elements in the political system (**216**). In the final assessment, the progress in administrative techniques was only one element in the governing of the state. Too much has been made, particularly by French historians, of the notion of a shift to a bureaucratic monarchy by 1715.

Administrative centralisation has been singled out by historians because it was the most visible new element in the monarchy, and they often equated the rise of the monarchy of Louis XIV with the rise of the modern state. In fact, there are three other new elements in seventeenth-century France which have recently been elucidated. The first is the financial system that grew up during the Thirty Years War, and was passed on to Louis XIV (**138, 134, 140**). It seems that the wars of his reign were financed not primarily by heavier taxation, but more by further sales of office and a system of loans guaranteed by the increased tax receipts. Attacks on local or social privilege* were often just a way of forcing a vulnerable group to buy off the assault (**16**). The second element is the growth of a large and better organised army, still much flawed, but now more loyal to the monarch than to the magnates, that was available to repress opposition. This was a consequence of Le Tellier's reforms and the 'military revolution'. Thirdly, the exploitation of mythology, propaganda and symbolism served to promote an image of monarchical power that itself deterred opposition. It tried to give legitimacy to the monarchy and its actions. None of these elements fits into what is traditionally regarded as 'centralisation', because they are not bureaucratic. Yet, if these elements are taken into account, we might agree that a different kind of centralisation of power was taking place – a slow shifting of the balance – as a prelude to the long and later process of bureaucratic centralisation.

Looked at in terms of institutional structures, France at the end of the reign still retained many elements of the *ständestaat*, the term given to a state made up of estates. The size of France and the strength of its provincial traditions, its provincial nobility, its legalism, meant that bureaucratic centralisation was never a real possibility without the prior destruction of these impediments. The localism, provincialism and corporatism of French society under Louis XIV were part of a whole culture not easily shaken by the monarchy. The institution of the intendants* was undoubtedly an important step for the monarchy, in helping to exert royal power in the provinces, but they were far from being the virtual administrators of France. The royal government was not yet simply a bureaucratic system, it was a judicial one with medieval roots: the intendants themselves were essentially judges. The dividing line between judging and carrying out the judgment was not one the *ancien régime** made much of, so the *police** of the intendants constituted an encroachment on the powers of many other corporations which consequently resisted them. Yet the vast majority of cases were judged (or administered) in the local courts: in seigneurial* courts, *présidial* courts, *cours des aides**, parlements* (**66, 67**). The correspondence of the intendants with the controllers-general shows them interfering only with the tip of the iceberg in terms of the volume of administrative and judicial business carried out in seventeenth-century France.

The thirty or so intendants* were a small corps amongst the perhaps 65,000 other royal officers in France. There were about 100 *présidial* courts, 12 parlements*, 13 *cours des aides** et comptes,* all conducting royal and provincial business. Their role, particularly that of the parlements, was also one of *police**. The Estates of the *pays d'états** were administrative bodies also. The vital part of governing that was based on patronage continued to flow mainly through traditional channels of bishops, courtly nobles and governors, although some intendants had good enough connections at court for them to play the same role. The transformation of the state by the intendants is simply a myth based on nineteenth-century historiographical preoccupations and on over-concentration on a limited body of evidence (**88**). They were neither all-powerful (there are cases of intendants being revoked when they bit off more local opposition than they could chew), nor were they very effective agents of centralisation, for their principal role was to observe, to report and to ensure the effective collection of revenue [**doc. 12**]. In this they were highly successful and were recognised by the ministers as indispensable.

France under Louis XIV was still ruled by the local elites, who were drawn together by royal policy and socio-cultural changes into a more unified whole. The provincial governors, bishops and intendants* were increasingly able to balance royal and local interests, by careful management and by the packing of provincial assemblies. The crown therefore worked with and not against the local elites in a new compromise. The rewards for the locals were the protection of the state against disorder, the right to spend some of the taxes in the locality on projects that honoured them, the help of the courtly notables with the advancement of their families, and the confirmation of their privileges* (**37, 64**). Socially, the crown and the elites closed ranks against the common people, who paid most of the taxes (**102**). But it was a stormy relationship that was not made in a day.

It is wrong to see the presence of the nobility at Versailles and the elaboration of court ritual as a ploy by Louis XIV to domesticate the nobility. This explanation reduces everything to an expression of the will of the King, when that is exactly what is in question (**204**). In fact, the court of Versailles, the elaboration of ceremonial and civility were all stages, perhaps the culmination, of processes stretching back to the Renaissance in France, and in Western Europe at large (**68, 69**). Louis was a product of these, just as he was also a product of the Spanish influence of his mother and the Italian influence of Mazarin. What we can say is that these traditions were not simply unconscious, but were reflected upon by political men, and therefore that Louis was aware of the potential of the system in which he lived.

A sombre picture of the men and politics of the era may appear cynical, but it is largely justified. The King and his ministers, however great they may have been, were men of their age. In that age saintliness was reserved for the church, not politics. To survive in politics it took family, patronage, wealth, cynicism and brutality. The monarchy was not a modern state imbued with respect for human rights and humanitarianism. The early modern state, the baroque state, was about power, royal power, *gloire** and dynasticism, and these presupposed very different sets of values from our own.

This book has not attempted to denigrate Louis XIV by exposing the underside of politics, by contrasting the image with the reality. That is not a new game to play, in any case (**33**). Care has been taken not to judge him in the light of our twentieth-century values. Much that Louis did was entirely to be expected of a nobleman of his era, beginning by the wars and the quest for *gloire**. It would be idle to expect him to have agreed with Leibniz's plans for a reordering of the world. If we can criticise him legitimately, it must be in the nature of an evaluation. This would use views put forward at the time, and those inherent in the ideologies of his own period. There was a tradition of criticism embodied by Fénelon and others who emphasised the limits of monarchical authority rather than its arrogant exaggeration. The policies of Louis XIV were responsible for the word 'despotism' gaining currency in France. Contemporaries were impressed by Versailles, and shocked at the same time [**doc. 7**]. Censorship was normal then, but since the time of Richelieu, there had been an attempt to suppress a whole tradition of writing on liberty. The royal discourse was increasingly orchestrated, to the extent that a blindness to other systems developed. Representative monarchy was not taken seriously and this explains the underestimation of Holland and England. Louis was partly responsible for this. He lived too long, and his ability to develop was limited. He did learn of course, and change in character, but the second half of his reign still saw him too inflexible. Although the negotiations with Austria in 1713 show that he could rethink his position, it was too late, the damage was done. Except in foreign affairs, the situation of the monarchy on the death of Louis XIV was disastrous. The debt amounted to perhaps 2,000 million *livres**. This was about thirty years' revenue from the direct and farmed taxes, based on Chamillart's average from 1701 to 1706 (**3**; Appendix 2). France was not sad to see an end to the reign. The foreign powers, sharing many of his assumptions, did not blame him for the Spanish War, and were more generous in their assessment.

The absolute monarchy of Louis XIV remained a limited monarchy. Louis and Colbert gave credence to the grandiose idea of a monarchy that had fewer restrictions, one in which the King really ruled by fiat through an efficient administration. It was an illusion, of course: they were themselves largely unsuccessful, but there are some signs that this administrative mentality was taking root in later eighteenth-century France. The truly extraordinary quality of Louis XIV was his talent for creating an image of monarchy, and identifying it with a style. He elevated royal grandeur to a new height as an art. In spite of his dreams of glory on the battlefield, he was above all a courtier king caught up in a theatre of power. He knew and understood the court and was able to keep a balance of favour and neutralise the adverse effects of faction.

In Louis XIV's own eyes, his real achievements were the establishment of his *gloire**, the addition of territory to France in order to create a more defensible frontier, and survival in an age of disorder. It is important to remember that there was nothing predetermined about the rise of the French state or the survival of the Bourbon dynasty in the direct line, or France's emergence as the foremost power in Europe. The task was a hard one. Louis began with a kingdom in temporary disorder, but could build on the foundations laid by his father and the two cardinals, Richelieu and Mazarin. It was never his intention to create a modern state, only to survive and secure the position of his dynasty in France and Europe. In the aftermath of the *Frondes**, the necessary compromise worked out in practice between the King and the aristocratic elite was favourable to the monarchy. Rather than substitute a centralised monarchy for the old structures, Louis used his awareness of patronage, symbolism, the financial system and the court to exploit the existing mechanisms of the state almost to their limits. Although he undermined the full economic recovery of France, and abused his position as monarch to develop his *gloire** at the expense of his people, he was successful in consolidating an ordered state and confirming the pre-eminence of the monarchy. In an age of iron this was no mean achievement.

Part Four: Documents

No brief collection of documents could cover every aspect of the period, and the following selection does not attempt to do so. I have entirely omitted foreign and religious policy. I have attempted, within the constraints of space, to convey to readers some very important but less frequently documented aspects of the reign, in order to provide material for a discussion of the political system. In addition to documents on the administration of the intendants* and the courts, I have provided evidence of the financial system, patronage and clientage, and the artistic policy. The translations are my own except where noted.

document 1

The condition of France in 1661

The years 1661–62 saw a particularly severe dearth in many areas with consequently harsh economic and demographic consequences. M. Bellay, a doctor in Blois, to the Marquis de Sourdis:

Monseigneur, I am quite sure that, in the 32 years that I have practised medicine in this province and in this town, I have seen nothing to compare with the desolation which there is, not only in Blois, where there are four thousand poor on account of the influx from neighbouring parishes and because of the poverty of the place itself, but in the whole country the dearth is so great, that the peasants lacking bread throw themselves upon the crows, and as soon as a horse or some other animal dies, they eat it; and it is certain that in the parish of Cheverny, a man, his wife and child were found dead without any symptoms of a disease, and only hunger could be the cause. Malign fevers are beginning to break out, and when the hot weather comes on top of so much damp and rot, these poor people, who lack strength already, will die quickly enough unless God works a miracle, we must expect a great *mortalité*. People are so poor that there was even a little barley in a boat that was left unsold, for lack of money to buy it. Our artisans are dying of hunger, and the town bourgeoisie is deeply troubled, for though they are full of goodwill to help these poor wretches, the great numbers make them unable to satisfy Christian charity. I have just learned that they have found a child at Cheverny who had eaten one of his own hands. Such happenings make our hair stand on end. Wine normally provided a livelihood for the people of this country, but it is not selling, and there are no horses to transport it, because of the high taxes. Finally, my Lord, every day I witness more sufferers who make me justly fear the worst, and, if this continues, I shall be forced to leave.

A reduction by half in the *taille*, and a delay in paying the other half until after the harvest has been requested, for the *élection* of Blois, Beaugency, for the Sologne, Romorantin and Amboise. The King has promised the Queen his mother, a reduction for the aforesaid *élection*.

A. Chéruel, *Mémoires sur la vie publique et privée de Fouquet, surinten-dant des finances*, 2 vols, Paris, 1862, II, pp. 325–6.

document 2

Contemporary views of Louis XIV

Louis at seventeen

As soon as he woke up, he would recite the Holy Office and his rosary; after this, his preceptor would arrive and have him study passages from the Holy Scriptures or the History of France. Getting up, he would go to his chamber pot, wash his hands, mouth and face. He would pray to God in the alcove where his bed was, with his almoners, everyone on their knees .... He would then go into a larger room where he would do his exercises: he jumped with admirable lightness, he used to have his horse set to its highest height and would jump onto it like a bird, making no more noise hitting the saddle than as if it had a pillow on it. After this, he practised arms and the pike.... Then, he would go up to see M. the cardinal Mazarin who lodges above his bedroom ... where every day a secretary of state came to report on business, about which, and about other more secret matters, the King was instructed for an hour or an hour and a half.

After mass, which he attended with the Queen [his mother], he accompanied her back to her suite with great deference and respect. The King would go back up to his bedchamber and change into apparel suitable either for hunting or for remaining at court. He was very easy to dress and dressed himself: his person was so marvellously well proportioned.

If, after dinner [in the afternoon therefore] an audience was held for the ambassadors, he gave it an attention that could not be surpassed, and, after their speeches were over, he would converse with them for a quarter of an hour very familiarly on the subject of those matters that concerned the friendship of their masters or of their countries.... It is charming to have the honour to approach his person to see and hear the admirable things which he is made of.... I have noticed such a great air of virtue about the King that none of those who have the honour of approaching his person would dare to swear or pronounce unseemly words.

After the Council, or a play, comes supper, at the end of which the King dances, the violins are present, the Queen's ladies and a few others. Then everyone plays games like telling a story: they sit down in a circle, someone begins a story and tells it until he is unable to continue, and then the next person takes up the tale and so it goes on from one to another and the tale is told, and some are so very pleasant. It being nearly midnight, the King says goodnight to the Queen and enters his bedchamber, and says his prayers and gets undressed before those present and converses with them very prettily; then, he bids goodnight, and retires to the alcove, where he sleeps. He sits down, on his way in, on his pierced chair where his closest servants converse with him ...

By Dubois, the King's valet and a gentleman, from **17**, pp. 64–6.

document 3

In the 1690s the former ambassador of Brandenburg, Ezechiel Spanheim, a somewhat hostile Protestant, wrote a critical appreciation of Louis, of which this is a short extract.

But alongside these good and splendid characteristics, which borrow lustre from the King's physical appearance and the fortunate successes of the reign, are others which do him less honour. Of these the first is a naturally limited intelligence which, as I have already observed, was little improved in the King's youth by those who had a vested interest in keeping him isolated from public affairs. He has since contrived to raise himself above this mediocrity imposed upon him by birth and education only by the changes which he chose to effect in the Government, by the necessity of curing the disorders after the death of Cardinal Mazarin, and subsequently by the prolonged and fortunate successes of his reign. Out of these conditions he has created for himself an art of ruling which depends less upon knowledge and reflection than upon contingencies and practice. It can therefore be claimed, with all due respect to the King and in spite of the extravagant eulogies of his panegyrists, that his is not a mind of the highest quality which perceives, ponders, resolves, undertakes everything without assistance, forms and executes the general plan – that quality which determines the true character of the heroes born to promote the glory of their age and the happiness of their people. To this limited capacity . . . must be added jealousy, a real but concealed hatred of anything which might challenge his grandeur, power, merit or become an object of public esteem or veneration. Consequently he regulates his plans and actions more often by principles of force and convenience than by good faith and justice . . . . Since he is absolutely jealous for his own authority and unreasonably sensitive of any threat to it, he can easily be led to accept the advice given to him and to adopt the measures proposed to preserve that authority, and therefore to attach more importance to considering the probable success of a policy than to reflecting on whether it is accompanied by all the necessary justice and good faith. Here is the fatal source, which must be more fully discussed, of the calamities and wars which have so often surprised and afflicted Europe, and which ravage it at this moment. Furthermore, since he is inclined to pose as the master rather than as the father of his peoples, he is rewarded with submission and dependence rather than affection and is untouched by an honest wish to relieve their sufferings. Hoarding pleases him even more than giving and there is usually some ulterior motive behind his charity and generosity: he gives for show rather than by choice. He is therefore as much inclined to ostentation as to thrift, and there is often profusion where there should be restraint, economy where there should be expenditure. It is necessary only to consider a contrast: on the one hand the twenty-four million paid for the château, gardens and waters of Versailles, or the Maintenon Aqueduct, where thirty thousand men worked for three years to carry water sixteen French leagues from a river to the reservoirs of the same Versailles; on the other hand, the misery of the poor people and the folk of the countryside, exhausted by the *tailles*, by the billeting of soldiers and by the *gabelles*. Alongside this should be considered the King's lack of care and tact in dealing with his friends and allies and in honouring the obligations which he has undertaken towards them.

E. Spanheim, *Relation de la cour de France* (**14**), pp. 38–9, translated in **15**.

document 4
Louis' regal style

Looking back on the reign from the time of the Revolution, the Baron de Bezenval remarked that Louis was a 'roi de théâtre', an appreciation confirmed by much recent research into ceremonial and display. The Duc de Saint-Simon here comments upon the transformation by Louis of words, gestures and a greeting into a valuable political currency.

In lieu of more tangible favours the king had a thousand subtleties which encouraged the court to hope for favour and which substituted for more substantial rewards, and which were intended to confer distinction or indicate a kind of chastisement: the misery of being invited to hold the candlestick at his *coucher*, of being included more or less frequently in the visits to Marly, and for the ladies, suppers in the Trianon when the king was there; of certain festivals throughout the year and other such trifles, all marked displeasure or distinction at a given moment, and, without constituting anything real, either sustained the hopes and the credit of the courtiers, or disappointed them. A look, a word from the king who was not free with them, were precious and would attract attention and jealousy. He was a king in every place, a king at every moment, a king who reduced everyone to respect and breathless anticipation, a king who by war and extravagance reduced the seigneur, be he grand or lowly, almost to dependence upon his generosity alone.

Saint-Simon, *Parallèle des trois premiers rois Bourbons*, J. de Bonnot, 1967, pp. 289–90.

document 5
Art and politics: Colbert's role as superintendant of the King's buildings

From the end of the year 1662, M. Colbert, having foreseen or already knowing that the King was to make him superintendent of his buildings, began to prepare himself for the exercise of this charge, which he regarded as much more important than it then appeared to be in the hands of M. de Ratabon. He realised that he would have to commission work not only for the completion of the Louvre, an enterprise that had been begun so many times but always left imperfect, but also to raise numerous monuments to the glory of the King, such as triumphal arches, obelisks, pyramids, mausoleums; for there was nothing either grand or magnificent that he did not propose to implement. He realised that he would have to have countless medallions struck to bequeath to posterity the memory of the great deeds the king had already done, and which, he could foresee, were to be followed by others even greater and more worthy of renown; that all these great exploits would have to be punctuated by entertainments fit for a prince, by celebrations, masquerades, tournaments and suchlike, and that all these should be suitably and intelligently described and engraved for distribution abroad, where the manner in which they are treated brings scarcely less honour than the events themselves . . .

Mémoires de Perrault, ed. P. Bonnefas, Paris, 1909, pp. 34–5.

document 6

The purpose of royal spectacle and the device

Louis XIV explained in his Mémoires *the purpose of public display and spectacles, and the meaning of his emblem:*

It was necessary to conserve and cultivate with care all that which, without diminishing the authority and the respect due to me, linked me by bonds of affection to my peoples and above all to the people of rank, so as to make them see by this very means that it was neither aversion for them nor affected severity, nor harshness of spirit, but simply reason and duty, that made me more reserved and more exact towards them in other matters. That sharing of pleasures, which gives people at court a respectable familiarity with us, touches them and charms them more than can be expressed. The common people, on the other hand, are delighted by shows in which, at bottom, we always have the aim of pleasing them; and all our subjects, in general, are delighted to see that we like what they like, or what they excel in. By this means we hold on to their hearts and their minds, sometimes more strongly perhaps than by recompenses and gifts; and with regard to foreigners, in a state they see flourishing and well ordered, that which is spent on expenses and which could be called superfluous, makes a very favourable impression on them, of magnificence, of power, of grandeur. . . .

The carrousel, which has furnished me the subject of these reflections, had only been conceived at first as a light amusement; but little by little, we were carried away, and it became a spectacle that was fairly grand and magnificent, both in the number of exercises, and by the novelty of the costumes and the variety of the [heraldic] devices. It was then that I began to employ the one that I have always kept since and which you see in so many places. I believed that, without limiting itself to something precise and lessening, it ought to represent in some way the duties of a prince, and constantly encourage me to fulfil them. For the device they chose the sun, which, according to the rules of this art, is the most noble of all, and which, by its quality of being unique, by the brilliance that surrounds it, by the light that it communicates to the other stars which form for it a kind of court, by the just and equal share that the different climates of the world receive of this light, by the good it does in all places, ceaselessly producing as it does, in every sphere of life, joy and activity, by its unhindered movement, in which it nevertheless always appears calm, by its constant and invariable course, from which it never departs nor wavers, is the most striking and beautiful image of a great monarch.

Those who saw me governing with a good deal of ease and without being confused by anything, in all the numerous attentions that royalty demands, persuaded me to add the earth's globe, and for motto, *nec pluribus impar* (not unequal to many things): by which they meant something that flattered the aspirations of a young king, namely that, being sufficient to so many things, I would doubtless be capable of governing other empires, just as the sun was capable of lighting up other worlds if they were exposed to its rays.

7a, pp. 134–6.

document 7

Versailles observed

(a) *Versailles was the focal point of the glorification by metaphor and allegory of the King and his achievements.*

Versailles, the splendid palace that I am about to describe, the admiration of centuries to come and the wonder of our own, will reveal to our most distant posterity that the protection of the arts, the levelling of mountains, the diverting of rivers or their rerouting through long canals, were amusements for Louis, and that this great King relaxed from his labours only by embellishing or surpassing nature.

Piganiol de la Force, *Nouvelle description des châteaux et parcs de Versailles et de Marly*, Paris, 1713.

(**b**) *Foreign visitors were astounded at the scale of the enterprise.*

The way to it is new, and in some places the mountains are cut down forty feet, so that now you enjoy it a mile in prospect before you come to it. It opens and closes in three courts, the more remotest, narrower and narrower, which is a fault, and is, as I was told, designed to be pulled down and made into one noble large square court, of the same order of building as that magnificent part is, which looks upon the gardens. The gilded tiles and roof have a marvellous effect in prospect. The esplanade towards the gardens and parterres are the noblest things that can be seen, vastly great with a very large basin of water in the middle, low walled round with white marble, on which are placed a great number of incomparable bronze vases, and large brass figures couchant, of the best masters in sculpture. It were endless to tell all the furniture of these gardens, of marble statues, and vases of brass and marble, the multitude of fountains, and those wide canals like seas running in a straight line from the bottom of the gardens as far as the eye can reach. In a word, these gardens are a country laid out into alleys and walks, groves of trees, canals and fountains, and everywhere adorned with ancient and modern statues and vases innumerable.

Dr M. Lister, *A journey to Paris in the year 1698*, London, 1699.

(**c**) *Not all foreign visitors were as impressed as Louis intended.*

The monarch as to his health is lusty enough, his upper teeth are out ..., and he picks and shows his under teeth with a good deal of affectation, being the vainest creature alive even as to the least things. His house at Versailles is something the foolishest in the world; he is strutting in every panel and galloping over one's head in every ceiling, and if he turns to spit he must see himself in person or his Viceregent the Sun with *sufficit orbi*, or *nec pluribus impar*. I verily believe that there are of him statues, busts, basreliefs and pictures above two hundred in the house and gardens.

Lord Montague, as cited in J. C. Rule (**41**), from *Manuscripts of the Marquess of Bath*, Historical Manuscripts Commission, 3 vols, London 1904–8, III, p. 192.

(**d**) *Saint-Simon, who lived in the château at Versailles, and was a severe critic of Louis XIV, was less impressed.*

He abandoned a town that was entirely built and whose position entirely maintained it for Versailles, the dullest and most ungrateful of all places without prospect, without wood, without water, without soil, for the ground is all shifting sand or swamp and the air accordingly bad.

He liked to subjugate nature by force of artifice and treasure. He built at Versailles on, ever on, without any general design, the beautiful and the ugly, the vast and the mean all jumbled together. His own apartments and those of the Queen, are inconvenient to the last degree, dull, close, stinking. The gardens astonish by their magnificence, but cause regret by their bad taste. You are introduced to the freshness of the shade only by a vast torrid zone, at the end of which there is nothing for you but to mount or descend; and with the hill, which is very short, terminate the gardens. The violence everywhere done to nature repels and wearies us despite ourselves. The abundance of water, forced up and gathered together from all parts, is rendered green, thick, muddy; it disseminates a humidity, that is unhealthy and evident; and an odour that is still more so. Their effects, which have to be closely husbanded, are incomparable but the result of the whole is that one admires it and flees .... From the garden side, one enjoys the beauty of the ensemble, but it is like looking at a palace that had once caught fire, and whose upper floor and roofs have not been replaced. The chapel which towers above it because Mansard wanted to commit the King to building another whole story, looks from every angle like an immense tomb. The craftsmanship in all genres is exquisite everywhere, the lack of good order complete, everything there is made for the gallery, because the King hardly ever went downstairs, and the rooms along the sides are inaccessible because of the single passage that leads to each of them. I might never finish upon the monstrous defects of a palace so immense and so immensely dear, with its accompaniments, which are still more so.

As translated in part in *Memoirs of the Duke of Saint-Simon*, by Bayle St John, 4 vols, Willey, New York, 1936, II, part three, pp. 232–3, with additions, and corrections by the present author.

(e) *Saint-Simon did, however, note a point of capital importance, that royal business was facilitated by having a large centre of government.*

[The King's] constant residence at Versailles caused a continual coming together of officers and persons employed, which kept everything going, and gave more access to ministers and their various business in one day than would have been possible in a fortnight had the court been in Paris. The advantage to his service of the King's precision was incredible. It imposed orderliness on everybody and secured despatch and facility to his affairs.

As translated and cited in **41**, pp. 42–3.

document 8

The politics of *gloire* and of flattery

As a part of the artistic propaganda of the monarchy, statues were erected in many provincial towns, often in the places royales. *The following extract from a long description of festivities was probably written by an intendant and was sent to court in a small printed edition.*

25 August 1687

The Ancients, wishing later ages to forget nothing about the great men whom Heaven had caused to be born from time to time, to serve as an example to others, were not content simply to celebrate their heroes in the immortal writings that they have bequeathed us; they also wanted to leave us a tangible likeness of them and thus, by means of statues and medals dedicated to them, delight our eyes as well as our minds. It is thus that we know today the features of those who lived more than two thousand years ago, thus it is that with the aid of these precious antique relics, we are able to form an idea of how those great heroes of the Greeks and Romans looked.

France, who has until lately been neglectful of these matters, is beginning at last to awaken, and to adopt the good taste of the Romans during a reign which is itself making the arts to flower; and as she has never possessed a hero so worthy of immortality as LOUIS-LE-GRAND, she has never displayed such a desire to emulate the Ancients by raising statues and striking medals to him, in order to preserve for the centuries to come his person and his features, and to allow those who follow us to admire the majestic air that inspires him and which is combined with so much goodness. Monsieur the Marshal de La Feuillade was the first to set us an example by commissioning statues. The great passion he has for the King's *gloire* has inspired him with a new project to help render him immortal: he has, in a display of the greatest magnificence, just set up a statue that will be an everlasting monument to the eternal victories of his prince, and also to his own zeal and gratitude.

Inspired by the desire to imitate him, the towns and provinces have immediately begged permission to raise similar monuments to keep before their eyes what they already have deeply engraved in their hearts. The city of Poitiers is of this number, and the better to display its love, has acted with the greatest of diligence, such that even if she is unable to surpass other towns, will at least retain the advantage of having preceded them in the deed. This is how it has come to pass.

The merchants, who make up a considerable body in the town, inspired by a rightful sense of gratitude for the benefits they receive every day from the King, who is the protector of Arts and Commerce, believed it their duty to provide outward signs of this gratitude by raising a statue to the King at the door of the building where they assemble to dispense justice. But M. Foucault, the provincial intendant, put forward the idea of making it into a public monument and setting it up in a square where, being the more visible, it would reflect greater honour on their zeal; they were pleased to adopt the advice he gave them, and wished to bear the cost of this monument themselves – a monument installed with all the success that was to be expected,

This monument is a full statue of the King in a noble and majestic pose, and is entirely suited to the hero it represents. The sculptor has excelled himself in portraying his expression and features. The King is represented in Roman dress, wearing a royal cloak hanging from his shoulders and strewn with fleurs de lys. The statue is set on a pedestal of great architectural merit, suitably adorned with carvings and ornaments. Four busts, portraying slaves of different conquered nations, support the four corners of the architrave.

From 'Mémoires Manuscrits de Foucault', Bibliothèque nationale, Ms Supp fr. 150, in P. Clément, *Le Gouvernement de Louis XIV*, 1848, pp. 239–41.

Patronage and clientage remained important forces in society. If they had been employed against the monarchy in times past, and might be again, they could also be harnessed to the monarchy as techniques of royal control.

document 9

Abbé Claude Fleury, *Devoirs des domestiques*

[A servant's] first duty is fidelity. It is the basis of all relations between men and particularly of relations in the household, which requires the confidence that a father of the family has in his wife, children and servants. Take away this confidence and human existence is nothing more than banditry and horrible disorder, worse than the life of the wildest animals.

In A. Franklin, ed., *La vie privée d'autrefois*, XXII.

document 10

The control of Burgundy by Condé

Nobody had acquired an office, either in the Parlement or any other jurisdiction without the mediation of M. le Prince de Condé, or that of Monsieur his father: nobody had acquired a benefice except by their nomination; all employment for the nobility was in their regiments alone, and all the office holders of the towns, mayors, aldermen, captains, lieutenants and ensigns, only obtained these popular honours by their intervention; in a word the Princes, father and son, had governed Burgundy with complete authority, for more than 20 years.

M-A. Millotet, *Mémoire des choses qui se sont passées en Bourgogne depuis 1650 jusqu'en 1668*, Mss de la Bibliothèque de Dijon, 492.

document 11

The following letter is a particularly good example of the tone adopted in letters dealing with matters of patronage and clientage.

Louis Antoine de Bourbon (Condé) to the Bishop of Avranches, 2 November 1696

I have just learned Monsieur, that the office of agent for the clergy has fallen vacant by the nomination of Monsieur the Abbé de Croissy to the bishopric of Montpellier; and the King having agreed that I might request it for Monsieur the Abbé de Langle, I beg you to be good enough to add your vote to that of my lords your colleagues to whom I am also writing. As I shall be most happy to be able to accord him some show of the particular friendship that I have for him, I will have a marked obligation to you for all that you might do on his behalf on this occasion; and I shall never pass by, Sir, any opportunity to show you my gratitude and the particular consideration that I have for you.

document 12
The duties of the intendants: the Instruction of 1663

The Inquiry that the intendants were asked by Colbert to carry out in 1663, the instructions for which became a document that the intendants subsequently referred to as a list of their duties, asked for information on taxation, commerce, the abuses of power, the elite and the church – it required them to observe and report on everything. Interestingly, and revealingly, one of his prime interests is the standing and patronage connections of all the members of the provincial elites. Note that in this stage of their development, the intendants are conceived of by Colbert primarily as observers, not the permanent officials they were to become.

[The instruction begins by asking for the basic information on the religious, military and civil areas of jurisdiction in France.] His Majesty desires that the [*commissaires*] draw up accurate memoranda on all that he wishes to know; namely:

ECCLESIASTICAL. With regard to the church, the name and the number of the bishoprics; the cities, towns, burgs and parishes which are under their ecclesiastical jurisdiction, their temporal lordships and the towns and parishes which come under them; particularly, whether the bishop is the temporal seigneur of the cathedral town; the name, age, estate and the disposition of the bishop, whether he is from the region or not, whether he usually lives there, the manner in which he conducts his pastoral visits; what influence (*crédit*) he has in his region and what effect he might have in difficult times, what sort of reputation he has amongst the people; if he has the right to grant the benefices in his chapter, if he is in litigation with it; his revenue; the name and the value of the benefices he confers.... It is necessary to record the name and the quantity of all the ecclesiastical institutions, both secular and regular ones, in the province ...

MILITARY. For the military government, which is the prime concern of the nobility, the second order of his kingdom, His Majesty wishes ... the masters of requests to begin the enquiry into the nobility by the name of the governors general, their health and marriage alliances in the province; if they are presently in residence; their good and bad conduct; if they are accused of taking money or vexing the people by some other means, if the accusations are valid; if the people complain about them; how much credit they have with the nobility and the people. And as the principal and most important task that His Majesty wants the governors to have is to strongly uphold justice and to prevent the oppression of the weak by the violence of the powerful, His Majesty wishes to be particularly informed of the past conduct of the said governors, in order to assess what he can and must expect in the future.... His Majesty desires to be particularly informed about everything to do with the nobility, namely: the principal families of each province, their marriage alliances, their wealth, the extent of their lands and their seigneuries, their habits and good conduct; whether they commit acts of violence towards the inhabitants of their estates, and, in the event that some important acts of violence have gone unpunished, he would like to know the details; whether they help or hinder the processes of royal justice in the bailiwicks and presidial courts; their credit in the region, both with other gentlemen, and with the people.

JUSTICE. With regard to justice, in the event of there being a parlement or some other sovereign company in the province, it is necessary that the masters of requests examine carefully, both in general and in particular, those who belong to it. As for the general aspects, you must look at its whole conduct during His Majesty's minority, what motives were behind its actions, and what means its principal officers used to influence it for good or evil. If its conduct was bad, find out if the reasons which have made it change since then provide strong enough grounds for believing that in a similar situation it would stand firm, or whether there is reason to fear that it might fall into the same error. And, as this is certainly the most important matter to examine in the province, it will be good and even very necessary to discover in detail the interests and qualities of the leading officers in these companies, and particularly whether those who led them down this path are still alive. Next you must find out the number of officers in each company, the name of the first president, of the other presidents, and the most influential men in the chambers; the good and bad qualities of the first president, his connections and his credit (*crédit*) in the company.... You must firstly find out in detail the way in which the company dispenses justice to the king's subjects; whether there is corruption or not; the causes of it and the men who are suspect. If some manifest injustice has occurred which has been noised abroad in the province and which has led to the oppression of the weak in favour of some friends, relations, or for some other equally disreputable reason, His Majesty wishes to be informed of it, just as he does of the length of trials and the excessive amounts required as presents, as much in the sovereign courts as in the lesser ones, it being important to know in great detail what relates to these two matters, which are a great burden to the king's subjects ...

BAILIWICKS. It is necessary to do the same thing with regard to the bailiwicks, seneschalcies and *présidial* courts; the number of officers in each seat of justice, the name of the seneschal, of the lieutenants-general and other officers, their personal merit and their credit with their companies and even with the people; what they would be capable of in difficult times; their manner of dispensing justice ...

FINANCES. For the finances, in the provinces which have a *cour des aides*, it is important to know the name of the officers, their merit and the connections they have in the provinces, particularly of the first president, then of the other presidents ...

ROYAL REVENUES. The king's revenues and what relates to them are to be examined. They consist of domains which have all been alienated, and which, consequently, produce no revenue; of farms of the taxes on entry and exit, of the *aides, gabelles*, of various other dues and farms, and of the tithes. For all five types of revenue, you must carefully search out how much His Majesty receives yearly from each province.... To acquit himself of all these tasks the *commissaires* must have a special and perfect knowledge of all that has to do with each kind of tax in particular, which is to say of the edicts, declarations and *arrêts du conseil*, and other orders which have established the dues, regulated the way in which they are collected, and the jurisprudence of the companies which have jurisdiction over them, together with the customs of each province.

AIDES (...)

GABELLES (...)

TITHES. You must discover, using your commissions, ... how much has been imposed in the last six years, so as to know the increases and reductions made by the king; then check if the *élus* have observed these ... finally discover the state of each parish in each *élection* [and investigate typical frauds and false nobles].

GIFTS, *OCTROIS* (sales taxes) [Discover the amount levied, and ensure that contracts to collect them are drawn up in future in the presence of the intendant.]

COMMUNAL DEBTS. To the article about the free gifts and sales taxes in the towns must be added information concerning the liquidation of communal debts, to which the *commissaires* must apply themselves wholeheartedly, there being nothing of such great consequence for the king's service and for the tranquillity of the people and of the inhabitants of the principal towns in the kingdom than to engage in discussion of these debts so as to reject and annul those which are not well founded, to reduce the interest on the others, and to get agreement on the way to pay them off by levies, either by poll taxes or by taxing goods, such that the king may have the satisfaction that in a fixed period which should be no longer than six or eight years the towns of his kingdom will be free of all debts ...

COMMERCE. His Majesty wishes to be informed of the changes which have occurred in the last forty or fifty years with regard to trade and manufacturing in each province of his kingdom ...

MARINE. *Commissaires* must find out the number of vessels belonging to His Majesty's subjects; let them strongly encourage the leading merchants and businessmen of the towns to buy ships and increase their number, to form companies for foreign trade, even to undertake long voyages; let them promise all the protection and assistance that will be needed . . .

MANUFACTURES. The same must be done with regard to manufactures, not only in order to re-establish all those which have been lost, but to establish new ones. . . . In the event that the *commissaires* think it might be necessary to grant some privileges, even some honours and some precedence in the towns either to merchants who make an effort to have vessels constructed . . ., or to the instigators of some large manufactures, His Majesty will grant them easily marks of his approval . . .

The said masters of requests should note that it is the king's intention that they make their inspections and carry out all the points contained in the present instruction in the space of four or five months, at the end of which His Majesty will send them orders to move to another province, leaving the memoranda and instructions on all the affairs begun but which they have not been able to conclude, so that they can be followed up by whoever succeeds them in the inspection; His Majesty desires that by dint of hard work and extraordinary application the said masters of requests should inspect the whole kingdom within seven or eight years and thereby render themselves capable of greater employments.

Clément (1): IV, pp. 27–43.

document 13
The influence of Madame de Maintenon

The political influence of Madame de Maintenon is hard to ascertain accurately. After the death of Colbert in 1683 the Colbert clan was under attack at court from the Le Tellier clan, and they had one of his financial clients, Bellinzani, who had supported Colbert's attack on rival financiers in the early 1660s, imprisoned in the Bastille in the hope of making him talk of Colbert's financial misdemeanours. Seignelay needed support at court.

At the death of M. Colbert, M. de Seignelay, being young, and not believing himself to have as yet sufficient credit in the eyes of the King to protect himself against the enemies of his father, looked to Madame de Maintenon: Mmes de Chevreuse and de Beauvillier were her close confidantes. The rank and character of Mme de

Maintenon required that she accept into her circle persons whose virtue and piety were above all suspicion; but M. de Seignelay did not take that route. Mme de Saint-Géran was a sort of favourite, she was greatly obliged to the house of Colbert, and M. de Savoy was all-powerful with her. M. de Seignelay used him to influence Mme de Saint Géran. It took no effort to persuade Madame de Maintenon to favour M. de Seignelay. If those ladies who have the favour of kings are necessary to ministers, ministers are not without their uses to the ladies; and Madame de Maintenon had yet another reason for choosing to favour him, which was one of the best where women are concerned; she happened to say one day that: 'You only had to look at these two ministers, to take the side of one against the other.' But as Madame de Maintenon could only influence the king by conducting herself with the greatest discretion and by hiding from him, with deep dissimulation, the influence she had over him, the protection that she accorded M. de Seignelay did not at first appear strong enough to save poor M. de Bellinzani.

Langlois (**71**): pp. 49–51.

document 14

Even a controller-general needed support at court, liable as he was to the attacks of faction. Here, Desmaretz makes a plea for continued backing.

Desmaretz to Madame de Maintenon, 26 July 1709

Allow me then to ask you, Madame, the favour of spending the time required in order to be the first to see the state of the kingdom and to comment upon it.

Allow me to remind you that having been entrusted with the control of finances in the month of February of last year, at a time when everything appeared hopeless, I arranged for more than 280,000,000 *livres* of expenditure, which have provided the means to re-establish and twice dispatch on campaign the most beautiful armies to be seen.

In the eighteen months since I was honoured with the place of Controller-General, the King has reduced the *taille* by 4,200,000 *livres*. The revenues from Flanders have gone down by nearly 3,000,000 *livres* because of the fall of Menin and of Lille. The King has ordered the supply of grain to Paris, and has provided funds to bring it from abroad for Guyenne.

Should one examine all that has happened since the beginning of the king's reign, and should one judge fairly whether any of my predecessors have had as little to work with as I have, will it not seem that I have done more than could have been hoped for?

The result of so much work and of so great an effort, is that my strength and my health have been exhausted by the excessive work. The courtier, worried for fear of being badly paid, designates my successors. 'I can no longer', he says, 'provide for the situation.' Without boasting, I might ask to be told who could. They are still saying that I am not to your taste, not your choice for the office. These are the words and sentiments of people of standing who are listened to. It is not difficult to calculate the effects they can have. Whose courage could stand up to so many afflictions and so many misfortunes? I must emphasise that the goodwill of the king has supported me, and that you Madame, have encouraged me with your own; but this support is more necessary than ever, if affairs are not to suffer in spite of all the care I take to maintain confidence.

Boislisle (**3**): III, p. 602.

document 15

Revolt in the Boulonnais in 1662

Louis XIV in his Mémoires *gives an explanation for the revolt in the Boulonnais.*

Two things appeared to me to be necessary in order to reduce the burden on the people. One was to reduce in the provinces the number of those exempt from the *taille* who, by this means, were passing on the whole burden to the poorest. To do this, every day I reimbursed a large number of small offices that were new and completely useless, and to which exemptions had been attached during the war, to help them sell.

The other was to examine more closely the exemptions that certain regions in my realm claimed to have, and which they possessed less by virtue of any title or great service, than by the accommodating ease of the Kings our predecessors, or by the weakness of their ministers. The Boulonnais was one such province. Its population has been used to war since the English war, and even has a sort of militia in various places in the governorship, which is fairly well trained and which answers the call to arms when needed. Because of this, they maintained that they were traditionally exempt from paying any sort of tithe. I wanted to levy a very small sum there, simply to make them recognise that I had the power and the right to do so. From the first, this produced a bad effect; but the use I made of the situation, although with pain and sadness, made it worthwhile in the long run. The common people, either alarmed by something that seemed novel, or secretly incited by the nobility, seditiously revolted against my commands. The remonstrances and leniency of those whom I had entrusted to carry out the matter, being taken for timidity and weakness, increased the tumult instead of calming it. Mutineers to the number of six thousand gathered together in several places: their anger could no longer be concealed. I sent troops to punish their sentiment; most of them dispersed. I pardoned without punishment those whose retreat bore testimony to a desire for repentance. Some, more obdurate in their crimes, were captured under arms, and they were abandoned to the law. Their crime merited death. I arranged matters such that most of them were only condemned to the galleys, and I would even have spared them this, if I had not thought it my duty to follow my reason rather than my inclination.

7a, pp. 145–6.

The King's comments are set in another context by the following letter.

document 16
Colbert to Machault, in charge of the repression

I must tell you in confidence, that this revolt might well give the king the idea of annulling all the privileges of the Boulonnais, which are very extensive, the population being exempt from the *taille, aides* and *gabelles,* and generally from all kinds of taxes, which is why it is of great consequence that you direct your inquiries and procedures in such a way that it will be clear that His Majesty will be entirely right and justified in carrying out this thought, should He determine to do so. I do not doubt that you will do this easily, and with your skill and your capacity to give matters the required appearance, that the scale of the occurrence in itself will furnish you enough evidence to give it such an appearance.

P. Clément, 'Les émeutes sous Louis XIV', *Revue des deux mondes*, LVIII, 1865, pp. 996–1021, p. 1000.

document 17

The elite connives in popular disturbances

An intendant blames the bourgeoisie for not repressing the revolt in the Bordelais, where in March 1675, after a rise in the tax on salt and the imposition of the stamp paper tax, the people rioted, shouting 'Vive le Roi sans la gabelle!'

De Sève, intendant, to Colbert, March 1675

What I find most annoying, is that the bourgeoisie has scarcely better intentions than the populace. The merchants who trade in tobacco, and who, in addition to the cessation of their commerce saw themselves burdened with large quantities of merchandise of this kind that the tax farmers were refusing to buy, and which they themselves are not permitted to sell to the public, are quite happy for the protests to continue so that they can continue to sell their tobacco with impunity. The other merchants had allowed themselves to be persuaded that after taxing tobacco it was intended to tax other merchandise. The foreigners with interests here are also fomenting disorder, and I do not believe that I should keep from you the fact that there have been very insolent things said about the former protection of the English, and that if the King of England should wish to take advantage of these sentiments and send a force to land in Guyenne, where the Huguenot party is very strong, he would, in the present state of affairs, pose a serious threat. Until now, Monsieur, the parlement has done as a body and so has each individual magistrate, everything that could be expected of the zeal of this company; but you know the inconstancy of the Bordelais.

P. Clément, 'Les émeutes sous Louis XIV', *Revue des deux mondes*, LVIII, 1865, pp. 996–1021, p. 1007.

document 18

Misery in 1709 could lead to urban riots

This year of 1709, since the month of January, wheat and other cereals have been very expensive. Wheat cost as much as 6 *livres* a bushel, barley 4 *livres* 10 *sous*, oats 50 *sous*, buckwheat 4 *livres*. It was even more expensive in the whole country, towards Rouen, after Troarn, which had led to much famine around about, particularly for the poor; this has given rise to a royal declaration and to several proclamations by the parlement, as a result, which have commanded every person to donate a sum of money, in proportion to his wealth in each parish, which has made it necessary to draw up lists in each parish of the town and in the countryside that were then strictly adhered to. This was not enough to stop some riots by artisans who lacked bread, because there were lay-offs in all the trades, particularly in the town of Rouen where they were on the verge of an outbreak of looting; for a crowd of nearly four thousand poor formed, and went to the home of the intendant to demand bread; not having found him, as he was in Paris, they wanted to sack his house, which they did only the next day. From there they went to call on his sub-delegate, whose furniture, linen and wine they pillaged, stole and broke up in the middle of the street. They dragged his carriages into the river to mock him. They then went to the home of the commissioner of police, whose name is Le Mercier, where they did as much as they had at the sub-delegate's. This disorder would have gone on if the bourgeois had not decided to put a stop to it. In order to do this, they closed the town gates and shops for two days. The courts recessed as well, the bourgeoisie were called to arms, and the mutineers were charged, when they were found in groups, with no quarter given. However, on the other hand, the parlement and the officials of the town brought some relief by giving them the means to live; and having found work for them to do things seem quieter now. We must hope that this tranquillity will last.

G. Mancel (ed.), *Journal d'un bourgeois de Caen, 1652–1733* (Caen and Paris, 1848), pp. 130–1.

document 19

(a) *The circulation of specie was very important both for national finances and commerce, and dried up in wartime. Colbert addressed this problem with his trade policies, as he explained to the King in a memorandum in 1670.*

The universal principle of finances must always be to remain vigilant and make use of all the care and authority of Your Majesty, in order to attract money into the kingdom, to spread it throughout all the provinces in order to procure for the people the means to live and pay their taxes. . . . The good state of finances and the increase of Your Majesty's revenue consists in increasing by every means the amount of coinage that circulates in the kingdom and in maintaining the right proportion necessary to each province ... in increasing money in public exchange by attracting it from the countries it comes from, by keeping it inside the kingdom by preventing it from leaving, while giving men the means to gain from it. As it is these three points that make for the grandeur, the power of the state and the magnificence of the King ... given that there being only a certain quantity of money that circulates in the whole of Europe and which is augmented from time to time by that which comes from the West Indies, it is certain and demonstrable that if there is only 150 million *livres* of coin in circulation, it is only possible to succeed in increasing the amount by 20, 30, and 50 millions by at the same time taking the same quantity from neighbouring states.... I beg Your Majesty to permit me to inform him that since He has taken over the administration of the finances, He has engaged in a war of money against all the states of Europe. He has already beaten Spain, Germany, Italy, England, where He has caused great misery and necessity, and has enriched Himself with their spoils, which have given him the means to do the great number of great things that He has done and still does every day. Only Holland still fights back with great forces: her northern trade ..., that of the East Indies ..., that of the Levant ..., that of the West Indies, her manufactures, her trade with Cadiz, that with Guinea and a host of others in which all her power resides and consists. Your Majesty has set up companies which will attack them everywhere like armies .... The manufactures, the canal between the two seas [du Midi] and so many other new enterprises that Your Majesty creates, are so many reserve corps that Your Majesty brings into existence to do their good duty in this war.... The tangible fruits of the success of all these things would be that by attracting a very large quantity of money into the kingdom through trade, not only would He soon succeed in re-establishing that balance there must be between money in trade and the taxes paid by the people but He would also increase both the one and the other, such that His revenues would increase and He would put His people in state to be able to help Him more significantly in the event of war or some other necessity.

Clément (1): VII, pp. 233–4.

(b) *If Colbert was perhaps wrong about the solution, he was right about the problem. Just after the end of the Dutch War (during which trade with the*

Dutch had been banned in Brittany) the Intendant of Alençon wrote to him.

There are almost no other coins in this Province, except 4 *sous* pieces, because all trade is now done with Paris: the cattle merchants, cloth merchants and traders in lace from Alençon leave their silver coins there and take back letters of exchange drawn on the receipts of taxation or on the salt tax, and they redistribute their money only in small quantities for their little purchases. The result is that we only ever see the same small change here, silver being almost never used. If the seaborne trade is re-established with the sale of grain and cloth, foreign coins will be brought in; but until now there is so little of that as to be not worth taking account of.

Translated from Meyer (**54**), p. 196.

document 20

The work of the intendants

Saint-Simon, anxious to renew and justify the political claims of the nobility, and to criticise the arbitrary power of the intendants, perhaps exaggerated their effect; however, his views have been influential.

The intendants who were still uncommon and not very powerful, were little employed before the reign of Louis XIV. The King and even more so his ministers, who were of the same stamp as the intendants, gradually increased their number, fixed the seat of their jurisdiction and increased their power. Little by little, they were employed to counter, then to reduce, and then to negate, the power of the provincial governors, of the military commanders, and of the lieutenants general in the provinces; even more so, they were used to negate the powers which well-born and distinguished seigneurs had on their estates and in their region. They restricted the bishops in the exercise of their temporal powers, opposed the parlements, and reduced the town councils to obedience. Their fiscal authority was very extensive; the arguments that result from all the different kinds of taxes and of laws, the power to impose a surtax (*taxe d'office*), their constant habit of protecting and humiliating the highborn and the lowly – of inciting and supporting the latter against the others – led to the most distinguished inhabitants gradually abandoning the provinces because they were not prepared to tolerate this new type of persecution, nor would they ever grow accustomed to courting the intendants so as to avoid, by means of the protection these men could provide, all the insults and affronts. The allocation of the *taille* and of the other taxes, resting firmly in their hands, gave them the power either to oppress or relieve parishes and individuals. Whatever claim, whatever dispute that arose between parties – whether a seigneur or no, a noble or a commoner – which was not taken before the local courts, was forwarded to the secretaries of state or minister of finance, and was invariably referred back to the intendants for their opinion – which, short of the occasional miracle, would always be followed. They thus acquired for themselves authority over all sorts of matters, leaving none either for the seigneur or anyone else; all who could do so abandoned their estates and their native regions to come and live in Paris, and at court, so that they might distance themselves from their loss of respect and from their fall, and here they would try to gain the credit and protection that would make the intendant treat them with respect.

J. de Bonnot, *Parallèle des trois premiers rois bourbons*, Paris, 1967, pp. 285–6.

From his first great Instruction to the intendants in September 1663 (see **doc. 12**), *Colbert unremittingly bombarded them with requests for information and orders to obey their instructions to the letter.*

document 21

Colbert to all the intendants, Saint-Germain, 1 September 1670

Monsieur, I am sending you the King's commission for the imposition for the *taille* for next year 1671; to which effect you will, if you please, take the trouble to send the enclosed to the bureau of finance and, after having collected them again, you will take yourself off to each and every *élection*, to allocate the burden between the communities, and keep a close watch to ensure that the distribution of the taxes is done with justice and equality. You will look upon this work as the most important task of all those with which you are entrusted, since it concerns the collection of the largest part of the receipts which sustain the expenditure of the state, and it is a question of rendering justice to the population in that matter which concerns them most, namely their fortune.

Take good care that the taxpayers should be all the more inclined to pay their taxes, in so far as they recognise the efforts you will have made, both to prevent all the chicanery which is only too common in this kind of matter, and to ensure that their tax is in just and true proportion to their wealth, by avoiding false declarations.

Clément (1) : II, i, pp. 72–3.

document 22

Colbert to M. de Creil, intendant in Rouen, Paris, 23 December 1672

The illness that I have had for the last eight to ten days, has prevented me from replying to your letter of the 6th inst. You should not fear the complaints of either M. d'Ocqueville or any other, about all that you are doing in the *généralité* of Rouen for the good of the King's service and the relief of the people. But you must be extremely careful not to encroach upon the jurisdiction of the judiciary for any motive other than the needs of the service; and even when this necessity compels you, you must make sure that no other motive is apparent – that is to say that all that you do must be free of suspicion, not only with respect to yourself, on whom you can rest assured that no shadow of suspicion will fall, but also with respect to your clerks. You must respect this rule, if you please, in your work, it being absolutely essential that those who serve the King in your post should give no grounds for complaint either directly or indirectly.

As M. Pellot is the principal magistrate in your *généralité*, it is necessary, for the King's service, that you entertain with him a close and perfect cooperation; and besides this general reason, you will gratify me with such behaviour, on account of the long friendship between him and me, and also because your collaboration will be useful for the administration of Rouen, to which you must both devote yourselves in the interests of the province.

In all matters, I beg you to listen favourably to the merchants every time they address you, and even to invite them to see you frequently to tell you about the state of commerce, and to search with them for the means of increasing and improving it; and when they need something that is within my jurisdiction, send word of it to me, if you please, so that I can express my views to you.

Clément (1): IV, p. 85.

document 23

If Colbert's letters, and those of his successors, testify to a war on abuses of the fiscal system at a local level, the fact that they reiterate the same problems shows that these same abuses persisted down to the end of the reign.

Colbert to M. Feydeau de Brou, intendant in Montauban, Paris, 5 August 1673

With regard to the abuses which are committed by the consuls in the reimbursement of the *estapes* [military supplies] to the persons who supply rations to the troops on their routes, and with regard to the embezzlement of the sums levied for the payment of these debts, I think that as far as the *estapes* are concerned, you should mete out an exemplary punishment to the most guilty in three or four places in the province, without carrying out too thorough an investigation, particularly because there is reason to believe that as soon as you have served punishment in a few places, all the other consuls, prompted by fear, will do all they can to make reparations for the wrong they have done and will give back what they have wrongly taken. Thus the punishment that you will mete out will repair the past and will create order in the future.

As for the embezzlement of the *octrois* [urban sales taxes] which had been allocated for the payment of the communal debts, I see no reason why you should not publish an ordinance along the lines of the project you sent me, particularly as it is a question of nothing more than the implementation of the orders in council which liquidated and regulated the payment of the aforesaid debts. But it is even more important that you devote yourself with particular application to ensuring that the said orders and your ordinance should be observed, since all these grand orders which are very useful for the public become useless and a burden when they are not observed down to the last letter.

Clément (1): IV, pp. 91–2.

document 24

As a rule, anyone dealing with money, collecting it, accounting for it or spending it for the royal service was likely to commit a host of petty or major frauds. Given the scale of the abuse, the royal response could only be exemplary punishment. In this letter the apparent control amounts to an enumeration of continuing abuses.

Colbert to the *Commissaires départis*, 28 April 1679

His majesty has ordered me to inform you that he wishes you to carry out this year a more precise visitation to all the *élections* and parishes of your *généralité* than you have done before, and with this aim I shall briefly reiterate the main points that you are to investigate. The first and the most important is the allocation of the *taille*; I am convinced that your diligence prevents many misdemeanours, nevertheless it is certain that, be it in the composition of the rolls or in the procedures for collecting the tax, or in the receipts that the receivers give the collectors, or in the constraints that are employed and the expenses that are paid for by the taxpayers, there are still many disorders which do not come to your attention, because of the care taken to conceal them by those who are guilty and who profit from them. The King wishes you to pay close attention to all these matters, so that nothing escapes your attention and so that you may impose the correct remedy.

Colbert to same, 5 May

The King orders me to add to the letter I have already sent to you, with regard to the inspection that you are to make, that His Majesty wishes that in each *élection* you choose three or four small or large towns to stay in for three or four days, and summon there the collectors of all the surrounding parishes and even some of the principal inhabitants, to gather information particularly about all that happens concerning the imposition and collection of the *taille*, so that, by means of this diligence and exactitude, you get to know all the abuses which are perpetrated, all the dispensations or under-assessments conferred on the rich as a result of interests or recommendations and which result in the oppression of the poor, the extraordinary or dishonest expenses charged by the receivers of taxes or by the bailiffs, and generally everything to the detriment of the people; His Majesty wishes that your knowledge might serve to render the imposition of the *taille* just and equitable and enable you to do away with all the abuses, and that you should draw up precise reports of the abuses that you discover, and of the remedies you have applied together with those for which you think it necessary to draw up some declaration or some regulation, so that His Majesty may set everything right in the light of full information.

Mémoires de N. J. Foucault, ed. Baudin, Société de l'histoire de France, Paris, pp. 418–21.

The parlements were managed rather than subdued and intimidated during this reign. Their jurisdiction was respected.

document 25

Chancellor Le Tellier to Marin, first president of the Parlement of Paris, 16 June 1682

I write to you to tell you that you should not have prevented the parlement not only from deliberating in order to choose the deputies to draw up remonstrances, but also to take a decision on the right punishment for the anger of the Sire Michaelis. You know that the Ordinance allows the companies to remonstrate after the registration of letters patent, and it is right to maintain them in that liberty.

Depping (2): II, pp. 240–1.

document 26

Chancellor Le Tellier to de Lavie, prosecuting attorney in the Parlement of Guyenne (Bordeaux), Versailles, 13 August 1685

I have received your letter of the third of this month; what you explained to me in it seemed to be very well argued; but the King does not willingly interfere with the established jurisprudence in the parlements, particularly when the good of his service and that of his subjects does not suffer from it, and when it is not contrary to the Ordinance. I think that there is no reason, for the present, to change the jurisprudence under which your parlement has lived until now.

Depping (2): II, p. 252.

document 27
Conflicts of jurisdictions between courts: Lebret, intendant of Provence to the Chancellor, 18 May 1692

It is true that the gentlemen of the Parlement frequently have disputes with the gentlemen of the Accounts about encroachments on their jurisdiction. Wishing to reconcile them, I have found much disposition on the part of the officers of the Parlement. But those of the Court of Accounts refuse on the grounds of two cases that they say are pending and about to be judged in council and which should decide all their disagreements; I believe all this could be no more than a pretext, and that they will not be reconciled, so long as they hope to obtain, by virtue of these squabbles, the transfer that they wish for of all their cases to a different parlement, just as they claim was recently granted to the Court of Accounts in Montpellier.

J. Marchand (**95**), p. 270.

Management and intimidation of the Provincial Estates: bluff, threats, backstairs negotiation, and compromise characterised crown-estates fiscal dealings. See also the documents translated in Mettam (32), ch. 3.

document 28
Letter from the Bishop of Béziers to Colbert, 9 January 1662 on proceedings in the Estates of Languedoc

S.A.S. [the Prince de Conti] will enter only on the 11th or 12th to make the request. M. the intendant, with whom I conferred today on this matter, thinks that the King must be granted 1,200,000 *livres* in the first deliberation, which will take place 7 or 8 days after the request. He hopes to bring the deputies around to it, and counts on all the bishops, barons, vicars general and envoys, and on several deputies he knows to be sound. My men will not fail him. In order to be more sure of success, it is necessary for us to agree about it in advance in a conference with the bishops and barons, about which there is no danger, because there is no one with a different opinion, and when there are one or two of the eight bishops and four barons, who might wish to treat the interests of the people with moderation, the majority will always win them over, and it is certain that in a conference the majority will be with what M. the intendant judges to be necessary for the King's satisfaction, and the others will follow this lead and will not want to appear to be the leaders of a contrary opinion. If the affair gets voted through at the sum of 1,200,000 *livres* in the first debate, we think that His Majesty's commissioners should come back the second time to declare that His Majesty cannot agree to this sum; it would be good to arrange matters so that the result of the deliberation was that the province gave itself over entirely to the will of His Majesty, after He had graciously permitted us to inform Him of the distressed state in which this province presently finds itself. Before carrying out this last plan, which can only be done in two weeks, it is necessary to examine it more closely, and sound out the disposition of the deputies, and even find out if the King approves.

The same to the same, 20 January

We deliberated yesterday on the King's business, and with almost one accord the gift of 1,200,000 *livres* was agreed. M. d'Alby and I were deputed to bear this news to M. the Prince de Conty, who told us that he could see from this first step that the Estates would give fuller satisfaction to the King. This unanimous and apparently unprecedented deliberation comes from the knowledge there is of the care the King takes to be informed of every detail of the affairs of his kingdom, from the care that M. le Prince de Conty has taken to persuade everybody, and the unshakeable firmness of those on whom His Majesty can most surely count . . . .

The fidelity of M. the Bishop of Alby and his zeal are well enough known for no one to doubt his intentions. Nevertheless, for some years now he has taken to have such confidence in the Bishop of Montauban that if he is not careful he will unconsciously come around to his attitudes, which are not to be trusted. The latter and M. de Montpellier had induced him not to opine for more than 1,000,000. But I made him understand that Messieurs de Mende, de Castres, de Saint-Pons, de Saint-Papoul and I, with the barons, namely, Polignac, Rabat, Ramont and my brother-in-law, would give our opinion for 1,200,000 *livres*, and that it would be accepted. M. d'Alby, who was in any case probably of our opinion, went to see S.A. to ask him to agree that he might opine for a million. S.A. paid him no attention such that he raised him to 1,200,000 *livres*, and the Bishops of Montauban and Montpellier, not daring to make figures of themselves, followed him, and the upper benches of the church and the nobility were unanimous in this vote.

The Third Estate, being much less well informed about the affairs of the world, and of the needs of the state, are normally inclined to spare the people, and the capitols of Toulouse are the ones who are used to appearing as the most zealous because they are at the head of the Third Estate. This year as a result of the preparation made by S.A., and of the particular dexterity of the Abbé Roquette who had persuaded one of them, they followed the opinion of M. d'Alby, and certainly by their example, thereby produced that unanimity, which is such a considerable advantage, and which I believe to be worth more than a hundred thousand *livres*, if they continue down the same road. I have much encouraged them, having assured the one who aspires to be part of the deputation to the court that his deed will win him more than 25 votes [*for him as deputy to Paris*]. The consuls of Narbonne who are creatures of the Archbishop opened the bidding at 800,000 *livres* and were followed by only five others. One opinion was for a million and some votes were void, and the upshot was as I told you at the beginning of this letter. You must believe, Monsieur, that my brother-in-law, M. de Gramant and I have done our duty, and that the details of this would be too lengthy; but without claiming too much for ourselves, I can indeed assure you that you were right to fear that the King's servants would find it difficult to obtain the sum desired by His Majesty; for the Province has suffered greatly, much more than can be expressed. To my mind, we are obliged to tell you this, and then to accord what the King requires, because he knows the good of his subjects better than they do themselves.

I think that M. the Prince of Conty will return to the Estates next Monday and that we shall be able to deliberate for the rest of the week. We must try to go to 1,500,000 *livres* and it will be an uphill struggle; because these two bishops, who are thoroughly disgruntled at having been obliged to go along with us are doing all they can to encourage the Third Estate to stick at the sum so far agreed; it is always easier to do harm than it is to do good; but we will take care to prevent them. After having made certain of the 1,500,000 *livres*, I think that all that can be done will be to have the money made payable monthly, and I think it will be impossible to get more than that. The good grace with which it has been granted should please the King; I, with my vote and my careful attention will do all that you would wish of me. The Bishop of Viviers allows himself to be led, and faithfully does what we tell him; as President he is acquitting himself better than expected, and he deserves a letter of approval.

Depping (2): I, pp. 63–6.

(a) *While it is certainly true that the Estates granted the 'free gift' with all appearance of obedience from the mid-1660s, the story may not be one of entire submission. The nobility and clergy were usually bought off with confirmation of their privileges – namely, those of the province – and the deputies of the Third Estate were intimidated or bribed into not opposing an increase of taxation that inevitably fell on the poor. This tacit bargain may have suited the elite – but there must be a suspicion that taxes were simply voted, and then not paid and argued about afterwards, as reductions were claimed. This document shows the non-cooperation of the taxpayers and of the elite, who are using their refusal of a loan to make their point, and extract concessions, after having granted everything the King asked for.*

The estates of Languedoc to the Duc du Maine and to the King, 17 November 1702

The estates of the province of Languedoc, always submissive to the will of the King and inspired by their usual zeal for all things regarding his service, have accorded His Majesty, in response to the request made by messieurs his commissioners, the sum of three million *livres* of 'free gift' and two million *livres* for the *capitation* of 1703, although according to their knowledge of what is still due for the *capitation* for the year 1702, they have no reason for hoping that they will be able to collect what is owed.

For the *capitation* of 1701, however diligently it has been possible to act until now, the sum of 55,000 *livres* is still owed.

For the tax of 1702, whose last tranche has fallen due, the sum of 1,557,000 *livres* is still owed.

And for the *capitation* of the said year which will end in six weeks and at the end of next December, the sum of 1,200,000 *livres* is still owed.

This clearly shows that the collection of the taxes and the *capitation* for the year 1703 will be even more difficult on account of the impossible situation in which the taxpayers find themselves, if His Majesty has not the kindness to grant a reduction proportionate to the state they are in.

The estates cannot have recourse to the expedient of a loan to relieve the *capitation*, because this kind of tax was imposed only in order to have it borne by every rank of person and even by those who do not contribute to levies on land or who have only noble property, and it would not be just that rural property, which is anyway only too burdened, should bear again the burden of these loans, which would be a double tax on them.

The estates cannot either raise a loan for the 'free gift' . . .

Doms de Vic and Vaissette, *Histoire générale du Languedoc*, XIV, p. 1606.

(**b**) *Basville, intendant of Languedoc, explained the peasants' reluctance to pay, and the ease with which the rich escaped their share.*

The people pay the *taille* only when they know that it cannot be avoided; as soon as they know that the reduction in their wealth will be followed by a reduction in the *taille*, it is to be feared that most of them will follow this practice only too much: their hope for the success of their reclamations will discourage them from paying. It is to be feared that with the taxes being set in future according to their ability to pay, the collector will find himself in difficulty in the case of a rich man whose wealth and effects are out of reach of the parish in which he is taxed.

Cited in F. Hinckner, *Les français devant l'impôt sous l'ancien régime*, Flammarion, Paris, 1971, p. 133.

document 30
The verdict of Clément on the royal administration

However conscientious the administrator may have been, the Controller-General was always of central importance. But the liquidation of the municipal debts proceeded slowly. Begun in 1661, twenty years later it had been successfully completed in only a small number of cases. . . . Inflexible rules and regulations, so many and such constant efforts to bring about results that were so partial, so disputed and so poorly established, prove just how difficult it was to bring about even the most useful of reforms, in spite of the despotic nature of the government. It is tempting to conclude that, during the old-regime monarchy, and even during that most brilliant and most autocratic period of the reign of Louis XIV, centralisation was somehow nominal and fictitious. With the exception of certain specific cases, for example, when it was a matter of bringing some rebels to heel, the mechanism existed but worked badly: the command was passed down the hierarchy, but was most frequently carried out tardily and partially. Even the most energetic ministers failed when confronted with the inertia of the *pays d'états,* of the communities and sometimes even of the governors or of the intendants, all of whom were assisted on the one hand by family connections or by important personages, and on the other by the distances made ten times longer by the poor roads and the unbelievable sloth of communications.

Clément (1): IV, pp. xxxi–xxxii.

Financiers and the monarchy

The following two brief accounts of the careers of financiers reveal the sorts of connections that existed between members of the same elite.

document 31

Michel Bégon de Montfermeil (1655–1728)

Bégon belongs to one of those well-to-do families of Blois with a lengthy involvement in finance; his grandfather and father, a *secrétaire du roi,* were both successively receivers of tithes for the *élection* of Blois. A marriage with the Charron de Ménars, another family in the town to which Colbert's wife belonged, greatly contributed to the rise of the Bégon cousins. Following his older brother, but with him, he made a career linked to the milieu of the administration of the navy. After having been general officer of the tax farms in Charente, Angoumois and in Briyage (in 1680) he became commissioner for gunpowder and saltpetre, for he was also a friend of François Berthelot. He then became sub-delegate in La Rochelle for his brother, who was then intendant of the navy in Rochefort. Next he became first secretary, in the bureaux of the secretary of state for the navy, to his relative Seignelay, and then to Pontchartrain, who was another scion of an illustrious family from Blois, and who also gave him his patronage. All his other family links brought connections with the financial world; he was related to the Loynes, to the Lubert and to the Du Pile families, all members of the Colbert clique and installed by him in financial and naval affairs. His brother François Bégon made a career as secretary to the treasurer general of the navy, then became Grand Master of the Rivers and Forests of the Blois region, while nevertheless taking part in various maritime ventures, which did not prevent his ruin.

Michel Bégon chose his wife from the same financial milieu; in 1684 he married Cathérine Guymont who was the daughter of a *secrétaire du roi* and payer of municipal *rentes,* and the sister of Paul Jacques Guymont, who was receiver-general of finance and related through his mother née Le Normant to that other great financial family. Michel Bégon was to strengthen his ties of friendship with the Berthelots through his children, since one of his daughters married a son of Berthelots de Pléneuf. Quite naturally, therefore, Bégon played a part in the business of finance, in particular during the War of the Spanish Succession, during which he participitated in fourteen government financial contracts. He also took a very active part in a host of economic activities; through his father-in-law he invested in the Saint-Gobain mirror works. But it was in maritime and colonial activities that he really showed his capacity; he invested in the African Company, the Cap Nègre Company, the Mediterranean Company, the South Sea Company and the Saint-Domingo Company. He is naturally to be found involved in numerous shipping ventures from 1681 to 1716, from the ports of Saint-Malo, Nantes, Dunkerque, and in Provence. Invited to share in the supply of rations and munitions, he became one of the pillars of the associations of military suppliers during the last war of Louis XIV's reign. However, his range of lucrative activities did not permit him to end his days in peace; from 1719 his financial situation was bad, he was compelled to sell his estate at Montfermeil, and when he died his heirs declined to accept his legacy of debts.

document 32

Jean Thévenin, the elder (died in 1708)

This man, who was to become one of the most important *traitants* [financiers] of the end of the reign of Louis XIV, was born into a Protestant family from La Rochelle which had provided, from the early sixteenth to the early seventeenth century, a long line of aldermen and mayors of the city. He was the grandson of a mayor of La Rochelle, who had been confirmed in his title of nobility by royal letter in May 1652; his father, an infantry officer, had taken the royalist side during the troubles in Guyenne, and in 1664 and 1665 had received letters confirming his nobility. He himself, after an obscure beginning, got involved in financial affairs at the beginning of the War of the League of Augsburg, and rapidly became, along with his friend and associate Paul Poisson de Bourvallais, the most important financial contractor of his time. Having become *secrétaire du roi* (1694–1708), then royal governor of Saint-Denis, and given the title of Marquis of Tanlay, he steadily increased his involvement in financial contracts during the War of the Spanish Succession until his death in 1708. During these last two wars of the reign, he participated in no less than 107 *traités* (financial contracts). But in addition to this financial activity he became involved in such lucrative enterprises as the provision of supplies to the armies and the management of large estates, for example those of the viscounty of Turenne. His extraordinary career owes much to the patronage that he never ceased to receive from the Phélypeaux, and notably from Pontchartrain, for whose estate at Villiers he was the financial agent. But the Thévenin family profited in a more general way from solid support in the ranks of high society; thus Philippe Thévenin, who was controller-general of French fortifications and one of Jean Thévenin's cousins, was a client of the Duchesse de Rohan, whose affairs he managed as intendant.

Dessert (**140**), nos. 30 and 509 (of 534) brief résumés.

document 33

The Dutch war as a turning point

Fénelon, who criticised the policies of Louis XIV from within the Christian tradition of limited responsible monarchy, located the origins of the later misfortunes in the ill-considered Dutch War.

Here is enough, Sire, to recognise that you have spent your entire life off the path of truth and justice, and consequently off the path of the Scriptures. So many terrible troubles that have been devastating all of Europe for more than twenty years, so much blood spilt, so many outrages committed, so many provinces pillaged, so many towns and villages reduced to ashes, are the disastrous consequences of that war of 1672, started for your *gloire* and so as to humiliate those makers of gazettes and medals in Holland. Consider, without deceiving yourself, with men who can be trusted, whether you can expect to keep all that you possess by the terms of treaties your enemies were forced to sign after such an unjustified war.

That war is still the true source of all the evils that France is suffering from. Since that war, you have always wanted to grant peace as a master, and impose the terms, instead of offering them with justice and moderation. That is why peace could not last. Your enemies, shamefully overburdened, thought only of recovery and of uniting against you. Is that surprising? You did not even keep to the terms of the peace you imposed with such pride. In the midst of peace, you have made war and made prodigious conquests. You have set up a *chambre de réunions,* to be both judge and party: that was to add insult and derision to usurpation and violence. You have sought in the Treaty of Westphalia equivocal phrases in order to acquire Strasburg. None of your ministers had ever, in so many years beforehand, referred to these terms in any negotiation to suggest that you had the slightest claim to this town. Such conduct has united and inspired all Europe against you. Even those who have not dared to declare themselves openly against you, at the very least impatiently hope for your loss of power and humiliation, as being the only hope for the liberty and repose of all the Christian nations. You, Sire, who could acquire so much solid and peaceful *gloire* by being the father of your subjects and an arbitrator to your neighbours, have been made into the common enemy of your neighbours, and you risk appearing as a harsh master in your kingdom.

Fom the *Lettre à Louis XIV,* written by Fénelon in 1694, but never shown to Louis (extract from **13**, pp. 145–6). It has been translated in its entirety in **18**.

document 34

It is interesting to note that Louis had advisers who could foresee the consequences the war might have, at the time of the war itself.

Courtin to Louvois, 16 September 1673

The King is doubtless the world's greatest ... prince. He can remain so with a peace settlement that all Europe would consider very honourable for him and very advantageous for his state. Thus I have trouble understanding why His Majesty wants to jeopardise this happiness and risk exposing himself to future troubles, which might indeed serve to show off his courage and valour but will doubtless be the ruin of his subjects ...

If ... one wishes to reflect in all seriousness and good faith on the internal affairs of the state, is it not recognised that funds are depleted, that most of the money has left the kingdom and will not return while war continues to ruin commerce? Can it not be understood that the taxes cannot be raised without violence that is very dangerous when we have so many enemies abroad? ... The authority that the King has exercised so absolutely (*souverainement*) up to this time, being attacked from without will weaken within the kingdom.

As cited in Ekberg (**152**), p. 175.

Glossary

Aides   Wide variety of indirect taxes, mostly on drink, levied by the state.

Ancien régime   Term invented by French revolutionaries to refer to the preceding regime.

Annuel   Annual tax of $\frac{1}{60}$ of the value of an office, also called the *paulette*, first levied in 1604.

Bailliage   Bailiwick; royal judicial circumscription, dating from the twelfth century, with court in first instance and appeal for relatively minor cases; headed by a *bailli* similar to a seneschal.

Bourgeoisie   Those members of the upper echelons of rural and urban society sufficiently well off not to work with their hands and possessed of privileges*.

Capitation   Direct tax on all men, including the privileged*, except the clergy, instituted in 1695, levied until 1699, and renewed with many variations and privileged exemptions from 1701.

Chambre de justice   Special financial court designed to claw back the gains of financiers, which sat from 1661 to 1665.

Champart   Tax in kind due to the seigneur*, averaging $\frac{1}{12}$ of produce.

Commissaire départi   Royal commissary appointed for specific tasks by a letter of commission, and thus a term used for intendants*.

Cour des aides   'Sovereign' court of appeal in matters of taxation.

Dauphin   The title given the heir presumptive to the throne.

Dixième   Royal direct tax levied from 1710 on wealth in land, offices and manufactures – an addition to the *taille**, as the privileged* managed to pay a very reduced amount.

Dragonnades   Use of brutal dragoons to pressurise Protestants into converting to Catholicism.

Election   Fiscal circumscription presided over by the official known as an *élu*, responsible for apportioning the *taille** and indirect taxes, and judging such matters.

Fermier   Leaseholder responsible for collecting seigneurial* dues for his own profit.

Frondes   Civil wars in France from 1648 to 1653.

Gabelles   Much hated tax levied on salt, of which a fixed minimum was supposed to be bought, which brought in 23,700,000 *livres** when leased in 1687. The price of salt varied greatly according to exemptions, privileges* and region or province.

General Farm   Lease in thirteen provinces of the principal indirect taxes, for which the Farmers General advanced the funds.

Généralité   One of thirty large fiscal circumscriptions which by 1680 have become the seat of intendancies*, with a bureau of finances and several *élections**.

Gloire   Reputation for noble deeds with contemporaries and posterity.

Intendant   Royal commissary empowered to oversee financial or military affairs in the provinces.

Liberty   A recognised legal exemption from an obligation, thus a privilege* – not our idea of natural rights.

Livre   Money of account, comprising 20 *sous*, and each *sol* 12 *deniers*, as in l.s.d.

Master of requests   A royal judge attached to the King's council; intendants* were usually masters of requests, and the office was venal*.

Noblesse d'épée   Nobility of the sword, military nobility.

Noblesse de robe   Nobility associated with the judicial profession.

Octrois   Urban sales taxes.

Officier   An official or officeholder in the royal administration.

Parlement   Sovereign – that is, final – court of appeal with wide powers of *police**; the Paris parlement had jurisdiction over 40 per cent of the realm; other parlements existed in a dozen provinces.

Parti Dévôt   Partisans of a Catholic foreign and domestic policy.

Partisan   Financier involved in a *parti* or *traité*, that is, a contract to collect royal indirect taxes.

Pays d'élection   Provinces whose royal administrative and fiscal area is composed of *élections**.

Pays d'état   Provinces with assemblies representing the three estates, which exercise financial and general administration.

Police   A concept which combines our separate ideas of justice and administration.

Privilège   A right or privilege, in the sense of an exemption from a general imposition; a social distinction. Privilege is a fundamental concept in the *ancien régime*.

Rente   Annual return on an investment; the investment itself, often in the form of a life annuity or a loan to the municipality, clergy or provincial estate.

Glossary

Seigneur   Lord, lay or clerical, noble or bourgeois*, possessing landed rights and *privilèges** of feudal origin.

Taille   The most important royal direct tax, either a hearth tax or a land tax, levied on non-noble persons or lands, depending on the region; it dated from 1439 and its proceeds were used as collateral for the extensive royal borrowing in wartime.

Traitant   A financier who has invested in the proceeds of an indirect tax, by a contract (*traité*), like a *partisan*.

Venality of office   Offices, both royal and corporative, were acquired by purchase as property, so officials were 'venal'.

Appendix 1: Chronology of the Reign

1638	5 Sept.: birth of Louis, later Louis XIV
1643	14 May: accession of Louis XIV on death of Louis XIII
1648	Peace of Westphalia with Austrian Habsburgs; war with Spain continues
1648–53	Civil wars in France: the *Frondes*
1651	Louis declared of age (at 13)
1654	Coronation ceremony at Reims
1659	Peace of Pyrenees with Spain
1660	9 June: Louis marries Maria Theresa, the Spanish Infanta; restoration of the Stuarts in England
1661	9 March: death of Mazarin; 5 Sept.: arrest of Fouquet; 1 Nov.: birth of Louis, the Dauphin; work on Versailles begins; first of 10 illegitimate children born of Louis; Assembly of Clergy insists on signature of Formulary condemning Jansenist doctrine
1661–64	War between Habsburgs of Austria and the Ottoman empire
1662	Louis buys Dunkirk from Charles II; Boulonnais revolt
1662–64	Quarrel in Rome between French ambassador and the Pope
1663–71	French Academies established
1664	Grand Enquête for Colbert by the intendants*; Port-Royal closed
1664–71	Hungarian struggle for independence, aided by Turks
1665–85	Council of Justice edits legal codes
1665	The Grand Jours in Auvergne; death of Philip IV of Spain, accession of Carlos II
1665–67	Anglo-Dutch War
1667	League of the Rhine renewed
1667–84	Canal du Midi constructed in Languedoc
1667–68	War of Devolution; by the Peace of Aix-la-Chapelle,

	France acquires 12 fortified towns on eastern frontier
1668	Peace of the Church. Secret Partition Treaty for Spanish empire in the event of the death of Carlos II
1670	Revolt in the Vivarais; occupation of Lorraine by French army
1672	Dutch War begins
1673	The controversy over the *régale* starts between Louis and the Pope
1675	Popular revolts in Bordeaux, and in Upper and Lower Brittany
1676	Affair of the Poisons
1678–79	Peace of Nymegen: France acquires Franche-Comté, Spanish towns in the Netherlands and Freiburg from the Emperor, and makes commercial concessions to the Dutch
1679–85	Persecution of the Huguenots and Jansenists
1680	Paris accords Louis title of Louis-le-Grand
1680–84	Reunions to claim dependencies claimed in treaties of 1648, 1659, 1668 and 1678, and annex them.
1681	Strasbourg pressurised into union; Casale, gateway to N. Italy, bought from Mantua
1682	Versailles centre of government; first grandchild (of 3 to survive) born; Four Gallican Articles
1682–99	Austrian Habsburgs at war with the Ottoman empire
1683	Death of Maria Theresa, the Queen, and of Colbert; Spain declares war to stop reunions; siege of Vienna by Turks
1684	Genoa bombarded; secret marriage of Louis and Madame de Maintenon; in June Luxembourg is occupied; Truce of Ratisbon
1685	Revocation of the Edict of Nantes, and the Edict of Fontainebleau; death of Le Tellier
1686	League of Augsburg formed between Spain, the Emperor and German princes, against Louis XIV
1687	Quarrel with Pope over franchise in Rome: occupation of Avignon
1688	Cologne election dispute; William of Orange invades England

1688–89	Occupation and devastation of the Palatinate by Louis' forces
1688–97	War of League of Augsburg/Nine Years War
1691	Death of Louvois
1693	Famine; reconciliation with Pope
1695–97	1701 onwards: the *capitation,* a new tax also on the nobility
1697	Peace of Ryswick: many reunions and Lorraine restored, Strasbourg kept, Louis recognises William III of England
1698	First Partition Treaty between France and Maritime Powers
1699	Feb.: death of Joseph Ferdinand, named sole heir (in 1698) by Carlos II
1700	March: Second Partition Treaty; Oct., Carlos makes Philippe, Louis' grandson, his sole heir; Nov., death of Carlos and Louis' acceptance of the will
1700–21	Great Northern War: Sweden attacked by Denmark–Norway, Saxony–Poland and Russia
1701	French occupation of barrier fortresses; July, Austrian troops occupy Milan; 7 Sept.: Grand Alliance against Louis formed; 17 Sept.: Louis recognises James Stuart as King of England
1702	William III dies; wife, Anne, Queen of England
1702–4	Revolt of the Camisards
1702–13/14	War of the Spanish Succession
1705	*Vineam domini*: a papal bull condemning Jansenism
1708–9	Terribly hard winter and subsequent dearth
1710	Port-Royal razed to the ground by soldiers; *dixième,* a new tax, instituted
1711	Tariff advantages of Dutch from 1678 extended to Britain and Baltic free cities
1711–12	Deaths of Grand Dauphin, then Louis' eldest grandson and his family
1712	Utrecht Congress opens
1713	Peace settlement at Utrecht; Sept., the papal bull *Unigenitus* condemns 101 so-called Jansenist propositions; negotiations with the Emperor at Rastadt
1714	Louis legitimises his bastards; peace with the empire
1715	1 Sept.: death of Louis XIV at 76 and accession of Louis XV, aged 5

Appendix 2: Revenue and Expenditure

The Revenues of the French Monarchy from 1661 & 1750, in *livres*

Year	Gross revenue	Net revenue	Expenditure	Deficit
1661		84 222 096	31 844 924	
1662	87 602 807	44 451 360	65 169 011	20 717 651
1663	88 906 002	51 121 802	46 545 737	+ 4 576 065
1664	89 243 319	53 718 105	63 067 766	9 349 661
1665	88 453 641	58 648 399	50 743 791	+ 7 904 608
1666	93 585 311	59 478 055	56 566 890	+ 2 911 165
1667	95 571 739	63 016 826	72 138 597	9 121 771
1668	102 276 084	64 540 607	64 864 415	323 808
1669	95 623 789	68 721 893	76 281 559	7 559 666
1670	96 338 885	70 483 834	77 307 798	6 823 964
1671	104 522 631	77 648 911	83 875 707	6 226 796
1672		75 579 154	87 928 540	12 349 386
1673		75 695 646	98 187 758	22 492 112
1674		80 859 235	107 803 861	26 944 626
1675		78 456 448	111 860 416	33 403 968
1676		77 764 377	110 071 449	32 307 072
1677		80 050 929	115 718 954	35 668 025
1678		80 692 534	109 930 506	29 237 972
1679		74 883 468	128 235 624	53 352 156
1680		73 232 700	95 967 860	22 735 160
1681		80 623 730	141 040 073	60 416 343
1682	102 053 341	79 153 656	199 624 654	120 470 998
1683	112 877 106	86 987 021	115 133 523	28 146 502
1684	135 622 831	106 250 432	160 910 276	54 659 844
1685	124 296 635	89 009 375	103 344 149	14 334 774
1686	124 981 531	93 661 576	94 430 648	769 072
1687	117 292 172	86 882 096	94 270 744	7 388 648
1688	117 733 378	87 725 673	109 132 060	21 406 387
1689	136 807 518	105 290 038	138 674 228	33 384 190
1690	141 145 372	106 642 985	149 319 381	42 676 396
1691	152 843 547	112 251 227	163 412 497	51 161 280
1692	149 269 725	112 564 170	178 654 754	66 090 584
1693	146 480 644	107 938 165	180 448 155	72 509 990
1694	145 967 156	102 534 295	161 671 948	59 137 653
1695	156 740 783	112 493 106	187 748 212	75 255 106
1696	156 926 206	111 456 025	162 467 613	51 011 588
1697	158 027 655	110 265 517	218 971 172	108 705 655
1698	122 358 842	72 944 653	211 036 685	138 092 032
1699	128 527 008	77 198 960	430 666 576	353 467 616
1700	119 241 039	69 041 711	116 145 000	47 103 289
1701	121 253 624	73 404 505	146 366 000	72 961 495
1702	115 294 002	54 931 155	160 416 000	105 484 845
1703	104 797 206	51 671 191	174 199 000	122 527 809
1704			161 568 000	
1705	78 349 508	66 550 685	218 642 000	152 091 315
1706	140 962 065	33 345 379	226 935 944	193 590 565
1707	145 510 829	80 464 843	258 230 000	177 765 157
1708	119 723 286	46 001 434	202 788 000	156 786 566
1709	116 803 427	42 339 606	221 110 547	178 770 941
1710	96 192 337	36 432 745	225 847 281	189 414 536
1711	102 112 510	38 962 962	264 012 881	255 049 919
1712	112 615 632	36 727 023	240 379 944	203 652 921
1713	115 005 439	36 116 275	211 697 672	175 581 397
1714	118 395 822	32 189 749	213 529 630	181 339 881
1715	165 827 000	69 730 000	146 824 000	77 094 000

These figures (from J.R. Mallet, *Comptes rendus de l'administration des finances du royaume de France*, London and Paris, 1789) are to be taken as approximate, given the difficulty contemporaries and historians have in arriving at satisfactory statistics from *ancien régime* sources. The above table is from A. Guéry, 'Les finances de la monarchie française sous l'ancien régime', *Annales, ESC*, 33 (1) (1978): 236. A more recent assessment of them, with graphs only up to 1700, is by R. Bonney in **135**.

Appendix 3: Louis XIV's Family Tree

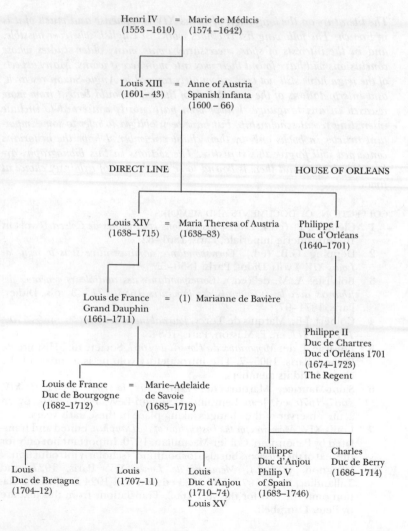

Henri IV = Marie de Médicis
(1553–1610)   (1574–1642)

Louis XIII = Anne of Austria
(1601–43)   Spanish infanta
             (1600–66)

DIRECT LINE   HOUSE OF ORLEANS

Louis XIV = Maria Theresa of Austria   Philippe I
(1638–1715) (1638–83)   Duc d'Orléans
                                          (1640–1701)

Louis de France = (1) Marianne de Bavière
Grand Dauphin
(1661–1711)
                                          Philippe II
                                          Duc de Chartres
                                          Duc d'Orléans 1701
                                          (1674–1723)
                                          The Regent

Louis de France = Marie–Adelaide
Duc de Bourgogne   de Savoie
(1682–1712)   (1685–1712)

                                   Philippe   Charles
                                   Duc d'Anjou   Duc de Berry
                                   Philip V   (1686–1714)
                                   of Spain
                                   (1683–1746)

Louis   Louis   Louis
Duc de Bretagne   (1707–11)   Duc d'Anjou
(1704–12)   (1710–74)
                                 Louis XV

Bibliography

The literature on the long reign of Louis XIV is immense and much of it is in French. The following list includes works in English wherever possible, and in the interests of space necessarily omits many older studies whose conclusions will have found their way into more recent works. Many aspects of the reign have still not been adequately covered by Anglo-Saxon research, and interpretations of the second half of the reign would benefit from more research in any language. I have been particularly concerned to include interesting recent scholarship, but have been obliged to refer to some important articles in books only by their chapter number. I hope the historians concerned will forgive this injustice. The sections in this bibliography are broad divisions, and there is bound to be an element of arbitrary choice at times.

COLLECTIONS OF DOCUMENTS AND MEMOIRS

1 Clément, P. (ed.), *Lettres, instructions et mémoires de Colbert*, 7 vols in 10, Imprimerie impériale, Paris, 1861–82.

2 Depping, G.B. (ed.), *Correspondance administrative sous le règne de Louis XIV*, 4 vols, Didot, Paris, 1850–55.

3 Boislisle, A. M. de (ed.), *Correspondance des contrôleurs généraux des finances avec les intendants des provinces 1683–1715*, 3 vols, Didier, Paris, 1874–97.

4 Colbert, J-B., Marquis de Torcy, *Journal inédit pendant les années 1709, 1710 et 1711*, ed. F. Masson, Paris, 1884.

5 Boislisle, J. de, *Mémoriaux du Conseil de 1661*, Société de l'Histoire de France, Paris, 1905–7. The introductory volume is a survey of the council and its members.

6 Saint-Maurice, Marquis de, *Lettres sur la cour de Louis XIV, 1667–1670*, ed. Jean Lemoine, Calmann-Levy, Paris, 1910. By an acute observer of the changes taking place in these early years.

7 Louis XIV, *Mémoires for the Instruction of the Dauphin*, edited and translated by P. Sonnino, Collier-Macmillan, 1970. Important not only for the text of the *Mémoires* but also for Sonnino's scholarly introduction.

7a Longnon, J. (ed.), *Mémoires de Louis XIV*, Paris, 1927, and Tallandier, Paris, 1978. The 1923 edition and 1924 English translation omit the text for the year 1662. Translations from this text are by Peter Campbell.

8 Bérenger, J. and Meyer, J. *La Bretagne de la fin du XVII siècle d'après le mémoire de Béchameil de Nointel*, Klincksieck, Paris, 1976. For both the text and a fine survey of Brittany in the introduction.

9 Comfort, W.W. (trans.), *The Clermont Assizes of 1665. A merry account of a grim court. Being a translation of Abbé Fléchier's mémoires sur les grands jours d'Auvergne*, University of Pennsylvania, 1937.

10 Rouvois, L. de, Duc de Saint-Simon, *Mémoires de Saint-Simon*, ed. A. de Boislisle, 43 vols, Paris, 1879–1930.

11 Dangeau, Marquis de, *Journal de la cour de Louis XIV*, ed. E. Soulié, 19 vols, Paris, 1854–60.

12 Sévigné, Madame de, *Lettres*, 3 vols, Pléiade, Paris, 1953–63.

13 Fénelon, *Ecrits et lettres politiques*, ed. C. Urbain, Editions Bossard, Paris, 1920.

14 Spanheim, E., *Relation de la cour de France en 1690*, ed. E. Bourgeois, re-edition, Mercure de France, 1973. An acute analysis.

15 Judge, H.G. (ed.), *Louis XIV*, Longman, London, 1965. Documents focusing on the government, very well chosen and edited.

16 Mettam, R.C. (ed.), *Government and Society in Louis XIV's France (1661–83)*, Macmillan, London, 1977. A fine choice of documents with excellent commentary. Essential.

17 Goubert, P., *L'Avènement du Roi-Soleil, 1661*, Julliard 'Archives', Paris, 1967.

18 Ranum, O.A. and P., *The Century of Louis XIV*, Macmillan, New York, 1972.

SECONDARY WORKS

The wider background

19 Pagès, G., *La Monarchie d'ancien régime en France*, 4th edn, A. Colin, Paris, 1946. Highly influential.

20 Campbell, P. R., *The Ancien Régime in France*, Blackwell, Oxford, 1988. In many ways a complementary volume to this book.

21 Briggs, R., *Early Modern France, 1560–1715*, Oxford University Press, Oxford, 1977.

22 Doyle, W., *Europe of the Old Order, 1660–1789*, Oxford University Press, Oxford, 1978.

23 Parker, D., *The Making of French Absolutism*, Edward Arnold, London, 1983.

24 Treasure, G.R., *Seventeenth-century France*, Murray, London, 1981.

General

25 Wolf, J.B., 'The reign of Louis XIV: a selected bibliography of writings since the war of 1914–1918', *Journal of Modern History*, XXXVI, 1964: 127–44.

26 Hatton, R., 'Louis XIV: recent gains in historical knowledge', *Journal of Modern History*, XLV, 1973: 277–91.

27 Church, W. F., *Louis XIV in Historical Thought*, Norton, New York, 1976. An illuminating guide to past interpretations.

28 Lavisse, E., *Louis XIV*, 2 vols, Tallandier, Paris, 1983. A re-edition of the relevant parts of the summary of nineteenth-century scholarship that was the *Histoire de France depuis les origines jusqu'à la Révolution*. Still fundamental.

29 Sonnino, P. (ed.), *The Reign of Louis XIV: essays in celebration of Andrew Lossky*, Humanities Press International, 1990. Unadventurous, apparently aimed at beginners. While some chapters are good, several disappoint.

30 Corvisier, A., *La France de Louis XIV, 1643–1715: ordre intérieur et place en Europe*, SEDES, Paris, 1979.

31 Méthivier, H., *Le Siècle de Louis XIV* (Que sais-je?) PUF, Paris, 1980.

32 Mettam, R.C., *Power and Faction in Louis XIV's France*, Blackwell, Oxford, 1988. An important perspective on the reign.

33 Goubert, P., *Louis XIV and Twenty Million Frenchmen*, Allen Lane, London, 1970. The first attack on Louis XIV from the perspective of the Annales school.

34 Goubert, P., *Clio parmi les hommes, recueil d'articles*, Mouton, Paris, 1976.

35 Labatut, J-P., *Noblesse, pouvoir et société en France au XVIIe siècle* (collected articles), Limoges, 1987.

36 Dessert, D., *Louis XIV prend le pouvoir. Naissance d'un mythe*, Editions Complexe, Paris, 1989.

37 Beik, W., *Absolutism and Society in Seventeenth-century France: State Power and Provincial Aristocracy in Languedoc*, Cambridge University Press, Cambridge, 1985. A fine, thought-provoking interpretation.

38 Lossky, A., 'The absolutism of Louis XIV: reality or myth?', *Canadian Journal of History*, 19, 1984: 1–15.

39 Rule, J., 'Royal ministers and government reform during the last decades of the reign of Louis XIV', in C. Sturgill (ed.), *Consortium on Revolutionary Europe*, University of Florida Press, Gainesville, 1973: 1–13.

40 Emmanuelli, F-X., 'Louis XIV et la Provence: les illusions de l'absolutisme', in 'Les provinciaux au dix-septième siècle', *Marseille*, no. 101, 1975: 49–58.

The following four books are all important collections of essays, with 20, 21, 24, 27, 32 and 37 good starting points:

41 J.C. Rule (ed.), *Louis XIV and the Craft of Kingship*, Ohio State University Press, 1969. An important collection of essays.

42 Coveney, P.J. (ed.), *France in Crisis 1620–1675*, Macmillan, London, 1977. Contains important articles by R. Mousnier and extracts from B. Porsnev, on popular revolt and society.

43 Kierstead, R. (ed.), *State and Society in Seventeenth-century France*, Franklin Watts, New York, 1975.
44 Hatton, R. (ed.), *Louis XIV and Absolutism*, Macmillan, London, 1976.

Biographical studies
45 Voltaire, *The Age of Louis XIV*, trans M. P. Pollack, J.M. Dent & Sons, London, 1926.
46 Lemontey, P-E., *Essai sur l'établissement monarchique de Louis XIV*, Paris, 1818. The main source of the nineteenth-century view. Reflected in Tocqueville's *The Ancien Régime and the Revolution* (1856 onwards).
47 Wolf, J.B., *Louis XIV*, Victor Gollancz, London, 1968; Panther paperback, 1970. First English full-length biography. Very much a biography, with little on France in general. Still better than Bluche (**49**).
48 Hatton, R., *Louis XIV and his World*, Thames & Hudson, London, 1972.
49 Bluche, J.F., *Louis XIV*, Blackwell, Oxford, 1990. Long, orthodox, with strong nationalist bias. Ignores most non-French research.
50 André, L., *Michel Le Tellier et Louvois*, A. Colin, Paris, 1942.
51 Corvisier, A., *Louvois*, Fayard, Paris, 1983. Covers all aspects well; important for the politics.
51a Rousset, C., *Histoire de Louvois et de son administration politique et militaire*, 4 vols, Didier, Perrin & Co., Paris, 1862–63. Interpretation superseded by **50** and **51**, but immensely valuable for information.
52 *Un nouveau Colbert. Actes du colloque pour le tricentenaire*, ed. R. Mousnier, SEDES, Paris, 1985. An outstanding collection of papers reflecting the latest research.
53 Trout, A.P., *Jean-Baptiste Colbert*, Twayne Publishers, Boston, 1978. A good brief introduction.
54 Meyer, J., *Colbert*, Fayard, Paris, 1984. A fine, sound study.
55 Langlois, C., *Madame de Maintenon*, Paris, 1932.
56 Dessert, D., *Fouquet*, Fayard, Paris, 1987.

Men and institutions
57 Chaussinand-Nogaret, G., *Les Financiers de Languedoc au XVIIIe siècle*, SEVPEN, Paris, 1970.
58 Mousnier, R., *La Plume, la faucille et le marteau*, PUF, Paris, 1970. Collected essays.
59 Mousnier, R., *The Institutions of France under the Absolute Monarchy*, 2 vols, University of Chicago Press, 1979 and 1984. A mine of information marred by a traditional institutional interpretation.
60 Antoine, M., *Le Conseil du roi sous le règne de Louis XIV*, Geneva, 1970. Chap. 1 is a good survey of the council in Louis XIV's reign.
61 Pagès, G., *Les Origines du XVIIIe siècle au temps de Louis XIV, 1680–1715*, CDU, Paris, 1939, reprinted 1961.

Bibliography

62 Harding, R.R., *Anatomy of a Power Elite: the Provincial Governors of Early Modern France*, Yale University Press, New Haven, Connecticut, 1978. Demolishes many myths about any decline in aristocratic power.

63 Harding, R.R., 'Aristocrats and lawyers in French provincial government, 1559–1648', in B.C. Malament (ed.), *After the Reformation*, Manchester University Press, 1980. Useful on early origins of the intendants.

64 Hamscher, A.N., *The Parlement of Paris after the Fronde, 1653–73*, University of Pittsburgh Press, 1976. A fine, detailed study which should lead to many revised judgements.

65 Hamscher, A.N., *The Conseil Privé and the Parlements in the Age of Louis XIV: a Study in French Absolutism, Transactions of the American Philosophical Society*, 77, part 2, 1987.

66 Hamscher, A.N., 'Parlements and litigants at the king's councils during the personal rule of Louis XIV: the example of *cassation*', in M. Mack and P. Holt (eds), *Society and Institutions in Early Modern France*, University of Georgia Press, London, 1991.

67 Parker, D., 'Sovereignty, absolutism and the function of the law in seventeenth-century France', *Past and Present*, 122, 1989: 36–74.

68 Solnon, J-F., *La Cour de France*, Fayard, Paris, 1987.

69 Asch, R., (ed.), *Princes, Patrons and the Nobility*, Oxford University Press, Oxford, 1991. Much of interest, with an especially fine introductory essay by Asch.

70 Elias, N., *The Court Society*, Blackwell, Oxford, 1983. An inspired sociological view.

71 Langlois, C., *La Cour de Louis XIV*, Paris, 1926. Studies three important memoir sources.

72 Le Roy Ladurie, E., 'Versailles observed: the court of Louis XIV in 1709', in *The Mind and Method of the Historian* (collected essays), Harvester, Brighton, 1981: 149–73.

73 Rule, J., 'The commis of the department of foreign affairs, 1680–1715', *Western Society for French History, Proceedings*, 8, 1980: 69–80.

74 Baxter, D.C., 'Premiers commis in the war department in the later part of the reign of Louis XIV', *Western Society for French History, Proceedings*, 8, 1980: 81–9.

75 Ricommard, J., 'Les subdélégués des intendants aux XVIIe et XVIIIe siècles', 3 articles, *L'Information historique*, 1962: 139–48, 190–5; 1963: 1–7.

76 Richet, D., 'La Formation des grands serviteurs de l'état', *L'Arc*, 65, 1976: 54–61.

77 Frostin, C., 'Le Chancelier de France, Louis de Pontchartrain, "ses" premiers présidents, et la discipline des cours souveraines', *Cahiers d'histoire*, 1982: 9–34.

78 Frostin, C., 'La famille ministérielle des Phélypeaux: esquisse d'un profil Pontchartrain', *Annales de Bretagne*, 86, 1979: 117–40.

79 Frostin, C., 'L'organisation ministérielle sous Louis XIV: cumul d'attributions et situations conflictuelles', *Revue d'histoire du Droit français et étranger*, 58, 1980: 201–26.

80 Mousnier, R. (ed.), *Le Conseil du roi de Louis XII à la Révolution*, PUF, Paris, 1970. A collection of useful studies of the personnel in the council, their careers and connections.

81 'Serviteurs du roi: quelques aspects de la fonction publique au XVIIe siècle', Special issue, *Dix-septième siècle*, nos. 42–3, 1959.

82 Hanley, S., 'Engendering the family: family formation and state building in early modern France', *French Historical Studies*, 16: 4–27.

Provincial estates have been comparatively neglected by historians of this reign, but see:

83 Major, J.R., *Representative Government in Early Modern France*, Yale University Press, New Haven, Connecticut, 1980.

84 Rébillon, A., *Les Etats de Bretagne, 1660–1789*, Picard, Paris, 1932.

Intendants
Most works on the intendants study them as institutions and there are no recent works setting them in the context of local power networks and clientage both at court and in the provinces. The provincial governors, commandants and lieutenants-general have been neglected for this reign (but see 62 and 32).

85 Moote, A.L., 'The French crown versus its judicial and financial officers', *Journal of Modern History*, XXXIV, 1962: 146–60.

86 Bonney, R., *Political Change in France under Richelieu and Mazarin, 1624–61*, Oxford University Press, Oxford, 1978. A well-researched view of institutional change before the Personal Rule.

87 Trénard, L., 'Les intendants et leurs enquêtes, d'après les travaux récents', *L'Information historique*, 1976.

88 Emmanuelli, F-X., *Un Mythe de l'absolutisme bourbonien: l'intendance, du milieu du XVIIe siècle à la fin du XVIIIe siècle*, Université de Provence, Aix-en-Provence, 1981. An important, iconoclastic, brief survey, drawing on his recent excellent thesis on Provence.

89 Fréville, H., *L'Intendance de Bretagne, 1689–1790*, 3 vols, I, Plihon, Rennes, 1953.

90 Livet, G., *L'Intendance d'Alsace sous Louis XIV*, Paris, 1956.

The following are the older studies:

91 Croquez, A., *L'Intendance de Flandre walonne sous Louis XIV*, Desclée and De Brouwer, Lille, 1912.

92 Dubuc, P., *L'Intendance de Soissons sous Louis XIV (1643–1715)*, A. Fontemoing, 1902.

93 Beaucorps, Ch. de, *L'Administration des intendants d'Orléans de 1686 à 1713*, Mégariotis Reprints, Geneva, 1978.

94   Godard, C., *Les Pouvoirs des intendants sous Louis XIV, particulièrement dans les pays d'élections*, Paris, 1901, reprinted Slatkine-Mégariotis, Geneva, 1974.

95   Marchand, J., *Un Intendant sous Louis XIV: administration de Lebret en Provence*, 1891. The most nuanced, sensitive regional study of an intendant.

96   Monin, H., *Essai sur l'histoire administrative du Languedoc pendant l'intendance de Basville*, Hachette, Paris, 1884.

97   Thomas, A., *Une Province sous Louis XIV, la Bourgogne*, Paris, 1844. An unjustly neglected study.

Social mobility, patronage and politics (see also 71–8)

98   'La mobilité sociale au XVIIe siècle', Special issue, *Dix-septième siècle*, no. 122, 1975.

99   Kettering, S., *Patrons, Brokers and Clients in Seventeenth-century France*, Oxford University Press, New York, 1986.

100 Kettering, S., 'Patronage and kinship in early modern France', *French Historical Studies*, 16, no. 2, 1989: 406–35.

101 Lefebvre, P., 'Aspects de la fidélité en France au XVIIe siècle: le cas des agents du prince de Condé', *Revue historique*, 250, 1973: 59–106. A fine case study.

102 Parker, D., 'Class, clientage and personal rule in absolutist France', *Seventeenth-century French Studies*, IX, 1987: 192–213.

103 Schalk, E., 'Clientage, elites and absolutism in seventeenth-century France', *French Historical Studies*, 14, 1986: 442–6, introducing a Special issue on patronage and clientage.

104 Bonney, R., 'Cardinal Mazarin and the Great Nobility during the Fronde', *English Historical Review*, 96, 1981: 818–33.

The following two articles on family fortunes provide an insight into the scale and scope of aristocratic wealth (see also 140):

105 Barker, N., 'Philippe d'Orléans, frère unique du Roi: founder of the family fortune', *French Historical Studies*, XIII, no. 2, 1983: 145–71.

106 Roche, D., 'Aperçus sur la fortune et les revenus des princes de Condé à l'aube du XVIIIe siècle', *Revue d'histoire moderne et contemporaine*, XIV, 1967: 217–43.

Economy and society

This section can give only a limited indication of the wealth of material available studied by the Annales school often over the 'long term'. Readers could also consult the works of R. Baehrel, C. Carrière, P. Deyon, P. Goubert, F. Lebrun, J. Meyer, M. Morineau, P. de Saint-Jacob, J.K.J. Thomson and M. Vénard – all authors of regional or urban studies. *107* summarises much of this work. The series of urban and regional histories *published by Privat (Toulouse) contains many distinguished essays on this period.*

107 Braudel, F. and Labrousse, E. (eds), *L'Histoire économique et sociale de la France*, II, 1660–1789, PUF, Paris, 1970.

108 Duby, G. (ed.), *Histoire de la France rurale*, II, Seuil, Paris, 1975.

109 Goubert, P., *The Ancien Régime, French Society 1600–1750*, Weidenfeld, London, 1971. Magistral and helpful.

110 Goubert, P., 'The French peasantry in the seventeenth century; a regional example', *Past and Present*, 10, 1956: 55–77.

111 Le Roy Ladurie, E., *The Peasants of Languedoc*, University of Illinois, Urbana, 1974. Now a classic regional study.

112 Jacquart, J., 'French agriculture in the seventeenth century', in P. Earle (ed.), *Essays in European Economic History, 1500–1800*, Clarendon Press, Oxford, 1974.

113 Bouchard, G., *Le Village immobile, Sennely-en-Sologne au XVIIIe siècle*, Plon, Paris, 1972. Explores the inter-relationship between all the various elements of village life. Excellent.

114 Dupâquier, J., *La population française aux XVIIe et XVIIIe siècles*, (Que sais-je?), PUF, Paris, 1979.

115 Cameron, R. (ed.), *Essays in French Economic History*, Irwin, Homewood, Illinois, 1970 by Zeller, Meuvret, Dupâquier, Morineau.

116 Meuvret, J., 'The condition of France, 1688–1715', *New Cambridge Modern History*, VI, 1970. See also his excellent collected essays: *Etudes d'histoire économique*, A. Colin, Paris, 1971.

117 'Aspects de l'économie française au XVIIe siècle', Special issue, *Dix-septième siècle*, nos 70–1, 1966.

118 Cole, C.W., *Colbert and a Century of French Mercantilism*, 2 vols, Columbia University Press, New York, 1939.

119 Cole, C.W., *French Mercantilism 1683–1700*, Columbia University Press, New York, 1943, reprinted by Octagon Books, 1965.

120 Schaeper, T.J., *The French Council of Commerce 1700–1715: a Study of Mercantilism after Colbert*, Ohio State University Press, Columbus, Ohio, 1983.

121 Schaeper, T.J., *The Economy of France in the Second Half of the Reign of Louis XIV*, Interuniversity Centre for European Studies, Montreal, 1980. Useful overview. Argues against government responsibility and modifies the usual bleak picture.

122 Scoville, W.C., *The Persecution of the Huguenots and French Economic Development, 1680–1720*, University of California Press, Berkeley, 1960.

123 Muchembled, R., *Popular Culture and Elite Culture in France, 1400–1750*, Louisiana State University Press, Baton Rouge and London, 1985.

124 Chartier, R., *The Cultural Uses of Print in Early Modern France*,

Princeton University Press, Princeton, 1988. Very stimulating on the new cultural history.

Popular revolt (see also articles reprinted in 41,42,43)

125 Porchnev, B.F., 'Les Soulèvements en France sous Colbert', in *Les Documents du commité culturel et économique, France – URSS, Histoire et géographie*, 5, Aug. 1954. Important because it lists the revolts and their sources.

126 Mousnier, R., *Peasant Uprisings in Seventeenth-century France, Russia and China*, trans B. Pearce, Allen & Unwin, London, 1971.

127 Salmon, J.H.M., 'Venal office and popular sedition in seventeenth-century France', *Past and Present*, 37, 1967: 21–43.

128 Garlan, Y. and Nières, C., *Les révoltes bretonnes de 1675*, Editions sociales, Paris, 1975.

129 *Les Bonnets Rouges*, coll. 10/18, Union Générale d'éditions, Paris, 1975: edition comprises A. de La Borderie, 'La Révolte du papier timbré advenue en 1675' (1884), and B. Porchnev, 'Les Buts et les revendications des paysans lors de la révolte bretonne de 1675' (1940, in Russian).

130 Beik, W., 'Urban factions and the social order during the minority of Louis XIV', *French Historical Studies*, 15, 1987: 36–67. See also Lemarchand in **43**.

131 Salmon, J.H.M., 'The Audijos revolt: provincial liberties and institutional rivalries under Louis XIV', *European History Quarterly*, 14, 1984: 119–49.

132 Pillorget, R., 'Genèse et typologie des mouvements insurrectionnels: La Provence de 1596 à 1715', *Francia*, IV, 1976: 365–90. Summarises his *thèse d'état*.

133 Joutard, P., *La Révolte des Camisards*, Gallimard, Paris, 1977.

Finance

134 Bonney, R., *The King's Debts, Finance and Politics in France 1589–1661*, Clarendon, Oxford, 1981. Important.

135 Bonney, R., 'J.R. Malet: historian of the finances of the French monarchy', *French History*, V: 180–233. Reviews the revenue figures of contemporaries, with useful tables and graphs.

136 Saint-Germain, J., *Les Financiers sous Louis XIV: Poisson de Bourvalais*, Plon, Paris, 1950. An excellent and readable introduction.

137 Matthews, G.T., *The Royal General Farms in Eighteenth-century France*, Columbia University Press, Columbia, NJ, 1958.

138 Dent, J., *Crisis in Finance: Crown, Financiers and Society in Seventeenth-century France*, David & Charles, Newton Abbot, 1973. Pioneering and well-researched, his conclusions prefigure those in **140** and **134.**

139 Dent, J., 'An aspect of the crisis of the seventeenth century: the collapse of the financial administration of the French monarchy (1653–61)', *Economic History Review* (2nd series) XX, 1967: 241–56.

140 Dessert, D., *Argent, pouvoir et société au Grand Siècle*, Fayard, Paris, 1984. Immensely important. Monumental.

141 Dessert, D. and Journet, L., 'Le Lobby Colbert: un royaume ou une affaire de famille?', *Annales, ESC*, 1974: 847–82.

142 Esmonin, E., *La Taille en Normandie*, Hachette, Paris, 1913, reprinted Slatkine-Mégariotis, Geneva, 1978.

Foreign policy

143 Zeller, G., *Histoire des relations internationales, III: De Louis XIV à 1789*, Hachette, Paris, 1955.

144 McKay, D. and Scott, H., *The Rise of the Great Powers, 1648–1815*, Longman, London, 1983. An efficient, detailed survey.

145 Bromley, J.S. and Hatton, R. (eds), *William III and Louis XIV. Essays 1680–1720 by and for Mark A. Thomson*, Liverpool University Press, Liverpool, 1968. Important chapters by Thomson, Hatton, Lossky and Rule.

146 Hatton, R. (ed.), *Louis XIV and Europe*, Macmillan, London, 1976. An excellent collection of essays.

147 'Louis XIV et l'Europe', Special issue, *Dix-septième siècle*, 123, 1979.

148 Lossky, A., 'The general European crisis of the 1680s', *European Studies Review*, 10, 1986: 177–98.

149 Sonnino, P., 'The origins of Louis XIV's wars', in J. Black (ed.), *The Origins of War in Early Modern Europe*, John Donald, Edinburgh, 1987.

150 Sonnino, P., 'The Marshal de Turenne and the origins of the Dutch War', *Studies in History and Politics*, 4, 1985: 125–36.

151 Sonnino, P., *Louis XIV and the origins of the Dutch War*, Cambridge University Press, Cambridge, 1988.

152 Ekberg, C.J., *The Failure of Louis XIV's Dutch War*, University of North Carolina Press, Chapel Hill, 1979.

153 Picavet, C.G., *La Diplomatie française au temps de Louis XIV*, Paris, 1930.

154 Picioni, C., *Les premiers commis des affaires étrangères aux XVIIe et XVIIIe siècles*, Paris, 1928.

155 Roosen, W., 'How good were Louis XIV's diplomats?', *Studies in History and Politics*, 1985: 89–102.

156 Roosen, W., 'The origins of the War of Spanish Succession', in J. Black (ed.), *The Origins of War in Early Modern Europe*, John Donald, Edinburgh, 1987.

157 Rowen, H.H., 'Arnauld de Pomponne: Louis XIV's moderate minister', *American Historical Review*, 61, 1956: 531–49.

158 Cuer, G., 'Pomponne, Feuquières et la Suède', *Revue d'histoire diplomatique*, 98, 1984: 193–219.

159 *The Peace of Nijmegen, 1676–1678*, International Congress of the Tricentennial, Amsterdam, 1980.

160 Zeller, G., *Aspects de la politique française sous l'ancien régime*, Collected essays, PUF, Paris, 1964.

Bibliography

Religion

161 Delumeau, J., *Catholicism between Luther and Voltaire*, Burns, London, 1977. An excellent general introduction.

162 Dompnier, B., *Le Vénin de la hérésie. Image du protestantisme et combat catholique au XVIIe siècle*, Le Centurion, Paris, 1985.

163 Parker, D., 'The Huguenots in seventeenth-century France', in A.C. Hepburn (ed.), *Minorities in History*, Edward Arnold, London, 1978.

164 Orcibal, J., *Louis XIV et les protestants*, Vrin, Paris, 1951. See also his article in **44.**

165 Quéniart, J., *La Révocation de l'Edit de Nantes*, Desclée de Brouwer, Paris, 1985.

166 Labrousse, E., *La Révocation de L'Edit de Nantes*, Payot, Paris, 1985 and 1990.

167 Garrisson, J., *L'Edit de Nantes et sa révocation*, Editions du Seuil, Paris, 1985.

168 Mettam, R.C., 'Louis XIV and the persecution of the Huguenots: the role of ministers and royal officials', in I. Scouloudi (ed.), *Huguenots in Britain*, Macmillan, Basingstoke, 1987, pp. 198–216.

169 Sedgewick, A., *Jansenism in Seventeenth-century France*, University Press of Virginia, Charlottesville, 1977.

170 Hamscher, A.N., 'The parlement of Paris and the social interpretation of early French Jansenism', *Catholic History Review*, LXIII, 1977: 392–410.

171 Taveneaux, R., 'Jansénisme et vie sociale en France au XVIIe siècle', *Revue d'histoire de l'église de France*, LIV, 1968: 27–46.

172 Martimort, A-G., *Le Gallicanisme* (Que sais-je?) PUF, Paris, 1973.

173 Sonnino, P., *Louis XIV's View of the Papacy, 1661–1667*, University of California Press, Berkeley, 1966.

174 Blet, P., 'Louis XIV et le Saint Siège', *Dix-septième siècle*, 123, 1979: 137–54.

175 Ceyssens, L., 'Autour de la Bulle Unigenitus: son acceptation par l'Assemblée du Clergé', *Revue d'histoire écclesiastique*, 80, 1985: 369–414 and 732–59.

176 Ultee, M., *The Abbey of St Germain des Prés in the Seventeenth Century*, Yale University Press, New Haven, Connecticut, 1981.

177 Ultee, J. Maarten, 'The suppression of fêtes in France, 1666', *Catholic History Review*, 62, 1976: 181–99.

Military and naval

178 Asher, E., *The Resistance to the Maritime Classes: the Survival of Feudalism in the France of Colbert*, University of California Press, Berkeley, 1960. A pioneering work.

179 Bamford, P.W., *Forests and French Sea Power, 1600–1789*, Toronto, 1956.

180 Baxter, D.C., *Servants of the Sword: French Intendants of the Army; 1630–70*, University of Illinois Press, Urbana, Illinois, 1976.

181 Symcox, G., 'Louis XIV's navy: problems and perspectives', in *Changing Interpretations and New Sources in Navy History*, R.W. Love (ed.), Garland, New York, 1980.

182 Symcox, G., *The Crisis of French Sea Power: 1688–1697: From the Guerre d'Escadre to the Guerre de Course*, Nijhoff, The Hague, 1974.

Political thought

183 Hazard, P., *The European Mind, 1680–1715*, Hollis, 1935, trans. in 1953, Penguin, London.

184 Klaits, J., *Printed Propaganda under Louis XIV*, Princeton University Press, Princeton, NJ, 1976.

185 Malssen, P.J.W. van, *Louis XIV d'après les pamphlets répandus en Hollande*, Nizet and Bastard, Paris (1936).

186 Ranum, O., *Artisans of Glory: Writers and Historical Thought in Seventeenth-century France*, University of North Carolina Press, Chapel Hill, 1980.

187 Rothkrug, L., *Opposition to Louis XIV*, Princeton University Press, Princeton, NJ, 1965.

188 Tréca, G., *Les doctrines et les réformes de droit public en réaction contre l'absolutisme de Louis XIV dans l'entourage du duc de Bourgogne*, Lille, 1909.

189 Kaiser, T.E., 'The abbé de Saint-Pierre, public opinion and the reconstitution of the French monarchy', *Journal of Modern History*, 55, 1983: 618–43.

190 Ellis, H.A., 'Genealogy, history and aristocratic reaction in early eighteenth-century France: the case of Henri de Boulainvilliers', *Journal of Modern History*, 58, 1986: 414–51.

191 Venturino, D., 'L'ideologia nobiliare nella Francia del antico regime', *Studi Storici*, 29, 1988: 61–102.

192 Spengler, J.J., 'Boisguilbert's economic views vis-à-vis those of contemporary reformers', *History of Political Economy*, 16, 1984: 69–88.

193 Leffler, P.K., 'French Historians and the challenge to Louis XIV's absolutism', *French Historical Studies*, 14, 1985, 1–22.

Art, literature, ritual, manners and symbolism
One of the most stimulating areas of new research has been the issue of the representation of monarchy and society through art, ceremonial and propaganda.

194 Adam, A., *Grandeur and Illusion, French Literature and Society 1600–1715*, Weidenfeld & Nicolson, London, 1972, and Penguin, London, 1974.

195 Mettam, R.C., 'Power, station and precedence: rivalries among the provincial elites of Louis XIV's France', *Transactions of the Royal Historical Society*, 38, 1988: 43–62.

Bibliography

196   Néraudau, J-P., *L'Olympe du Roi-Soleil, ou comment la mythologie et l'Antiquité furent mises au service de l'idéologie monarchique sous Louis XIV ...*, Les Belles Lettres, Paris, 1986. Comprehensive. The best introduction to this subject.

197   Christout, M-F., *Le Ballet de cour de Louis XIV, 1643–1672*, Picard, Paris, 1967.

198   Fogel, M., *Les Cérémonies de l'information dans la France du XVIe au XVIIIe siècle*, Fayard, Paris, 1989.

199   Moine, M-C., *Les Fêtes à la cour du Roi-Soleil, 1653–1715*, Lanore, Paris, 1984.

200   McGowan, M., 'Racine's lieu théâtral', in W.D. Holworth *et al.* (eds), *Form and Meaning*, Avebury, Amersham, 1982: 166–86.

201   Marin, L., *Portrait of the King*, Macmillan, London, 1988.

202   Ferrier-Caverivière, N., *L'image de Louis XIV dans la littérature française de 1660 à 1715*, PUF, Paris, 1981. Important.

203   Ferrier-Caverivière, N., 'Louis XIV et ses symboles dans l'histoire métallique du règne de Louis-le-Grand', *Dix-septiéme siécle*, 134, 1982: 19–30.

204   Giesey, R., 'The King imagined', in K. Baker (ed.), *The French Revolution and the Creation of Modern Political Culture:* vol. I, *The Ancien Régime*, Pergamon, Oxford, 1988: 141–60.

205   Sabatier, G., 'Representare il principe, figurer l'état. Les programmes iconographiques d'état en France et en Italie du XVe au XVIIe siècle' in *Genèse de l'état moderne: Bilans et perspectives*, CNRS, Paris, 1990: 247–58.

206   Ranum, O., *Paris in the Age of Absolutism*, Wiley, Chichester and New York, 1968.

207   Ranum, O., 'Courtesy, absolutism and the rise of the French state, 1630–1660', *Journal of Modern History*, 52, 1980: 426–51.

208   Isherwood, R., *Music in the Service of the King*, Cornell University Press, Ithaca, NY, and London, 1973.

209   *The Sun King, Louis XIV and his World*, Louisiana State Museum exhibition catalogue, New Orleans, 1984. A fine collection of essays with well-catalogued illustrations. Extremely worthwhile.

210   Apostolides, J-M., *Le Roi-machine: spectacle et politique au temps de Louis XIV*, Editions de Minuit, Paris, 1981. A fascinating theme seriously marred by presuppositions about absolutism and society.

211   Autin, J., *Louis XIV architecte*, Lanore, Paris, 1981.

212   Bottineau, Y., *Versailles, miroir des princes*, Arthaud, Paris, 1989. Scholarly and up-to-date.

213   Himmelfarb, H., 'Versailles, fonctions et légendes', in *Les lieux de mémoire*, P. Nora (ed.), vol. II, *La Nation*, Paris, 1986: 235–92. See also E. Pommier, 'Versailles, l'image du souverain', *ibid.*: 193–234.

214   Ross, S., 'Painting the passions: Charles Le Brun's *Conférence sur l'expression*', *Journal of the History of Ideas*, 45, 1984: 25–47.

215 Adams, W.H., *The French Garden*, 1500–1800, Brazillier, New York, 1979. An excellent introduction.

Additions
216 Campbell, P.R., *Power and Politics in France in the Age of Fleury 1723–45* (Provisional title), London, Routledge, 1994. Sets the supposed changes of the reign of Louis XIV in a longer and critical perspective.

217 Markovitch, J., *Histoire des industries françaises*, Paris, 1976. Contains important research for a reassessment.

218 Daire, E. (ed.), *Economistes financiers du XVIIIe siècle*, 1843, Slatkine repr., Geneva, 1971. Contains works by Vauban, Boisguilbert, Law, Melon and Dutot.

219 Blomfield, Sir R., *Sebastien le Prestre de Vauban, 1633–1707*, London, 1938, and Barnes & Noble, New York, 1971.

220 Burke, P., *The Fabrication of Louis XIV*, Yale University Press, New Haven and London, 1992. Surprisingly brief but too theoretical.

Index